FOR ORGANS, PIANOS & ELECTRONIC KEYBOARDS

E-Z PLAY TODAY
71

21 Top Hits

ISBN 978-1-4950-9664-8

HAL•LEONARD®

7777 W. BLUEMOUND RD. P.O. BOX 13819 MILWAUKEE, WI 53213

E-Z Play® Today Music Notation © 1975 by HAL LEONARD LLC
E-Z PLAY and EASY ELECTRONIC KEYBOARD MUSIC are registered trademarks of HAL LEONARD LLC.

Visit Hal Leonard Online at
www.halleonard.com

Blank Space

Registration 7
Rhythm: Pops or Rock

Words and Music by Taylor Swift,
Max Martin and Shellback

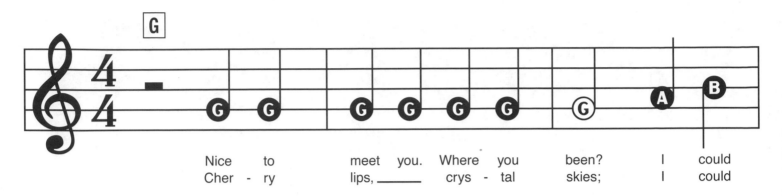

Nice to meet you. Where you been? I could
Cher - ry lips, _____ crys - tal skies; I could

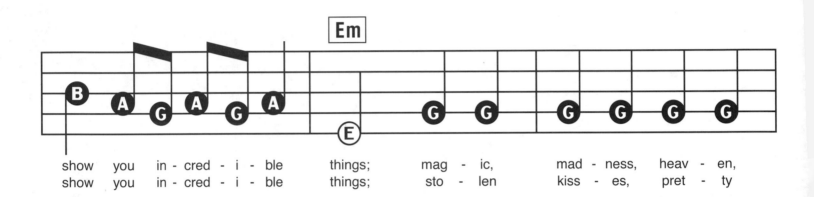

show you in - cred - i - ble things; mag - ic, mad - ness, heav - en,
show you in - cred - i - ble things; sto - len kiss - es, pret - ty

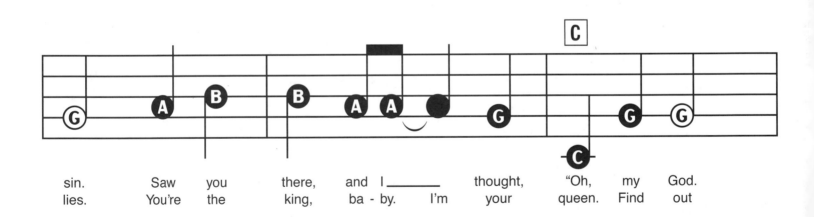

sin. Saw you there, and I _____ thought, "Oh, my God.
lies. You're the king, ba - by. I'm your queen. Find out

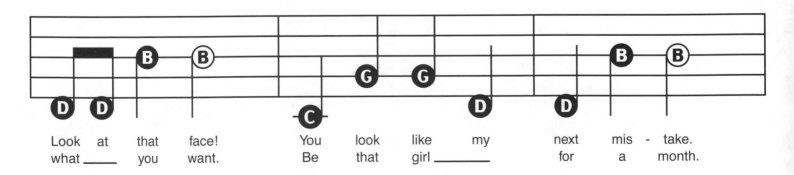

Look at that face! You look like my next mis - take.
what _____ you want. Be that girl _____ for a month.

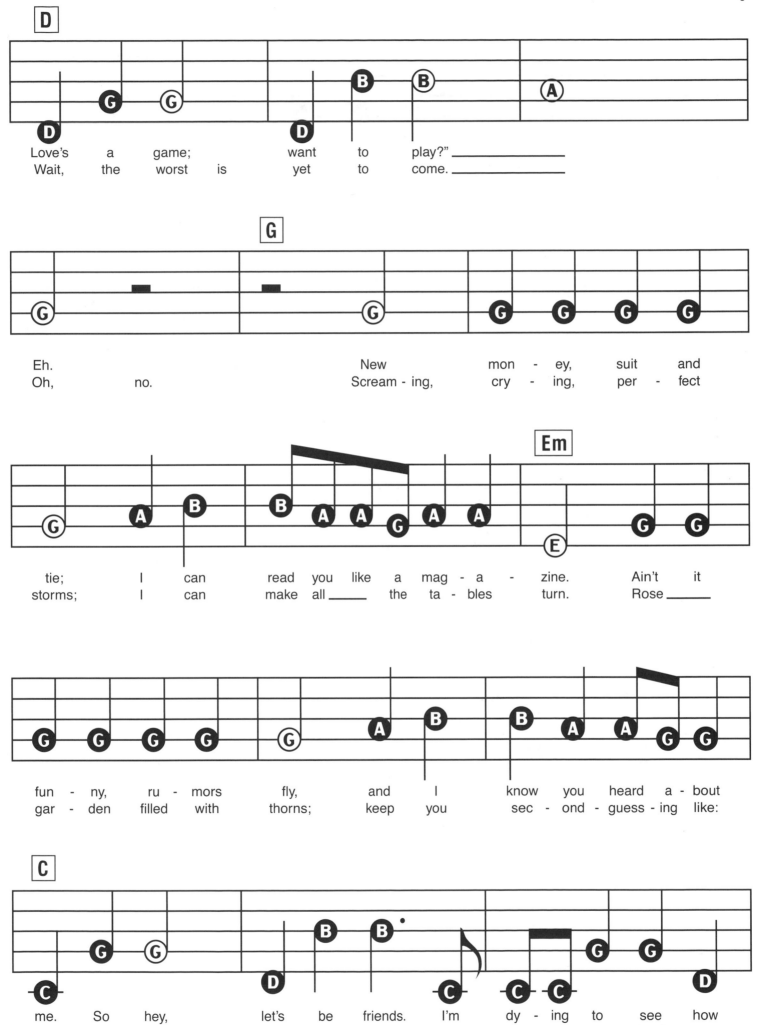

4

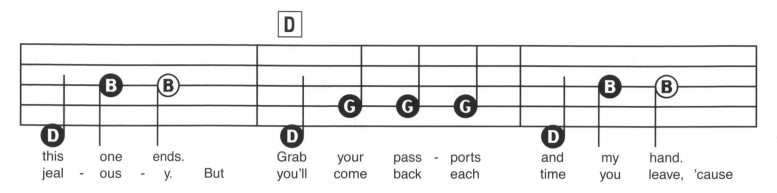

this one ends. Grab your pass - ports and my hand.
jeal - ous - y. But you'll come back each time you leave, 'cause

N.C.

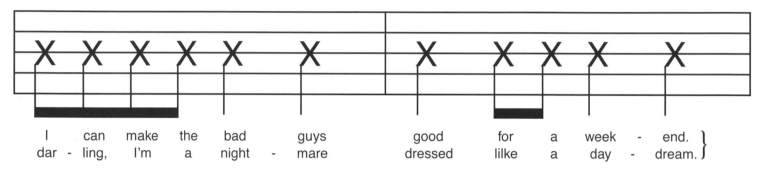

I can make the bad guys good for a week - end.
dar - ling, I'm a night - mare dressed like a day - dream.

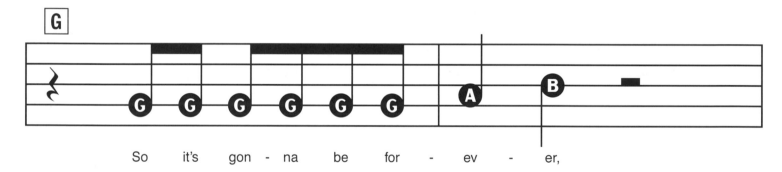

So it's gon - na be for - ev - er,

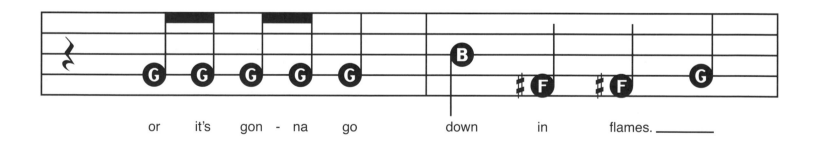

or it's gon - na go down in flames. _____

Em

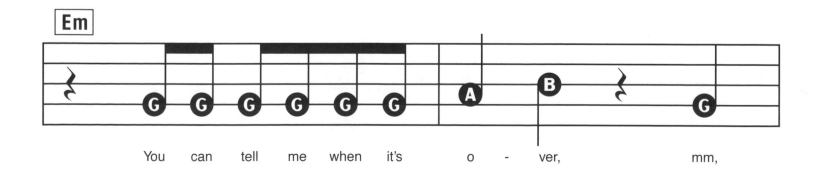

You can tell me when it's o - ver, mm,

5

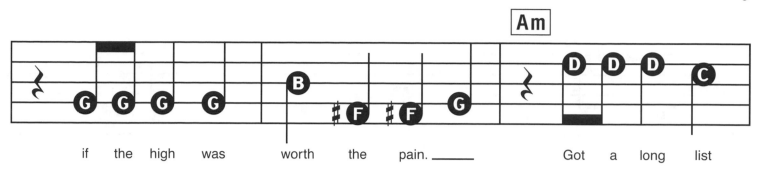

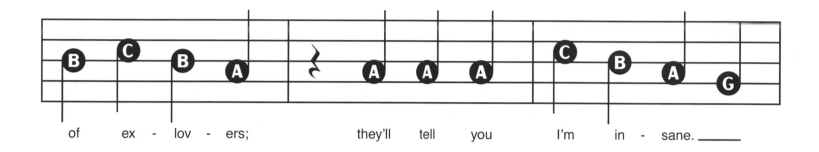

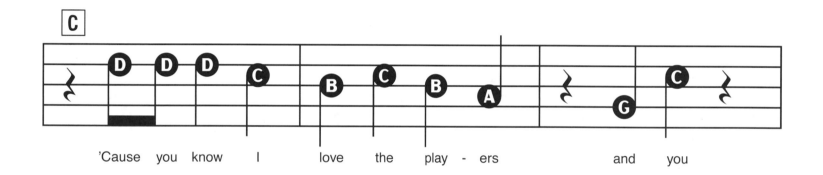

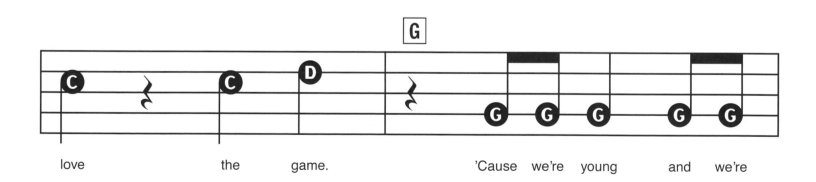

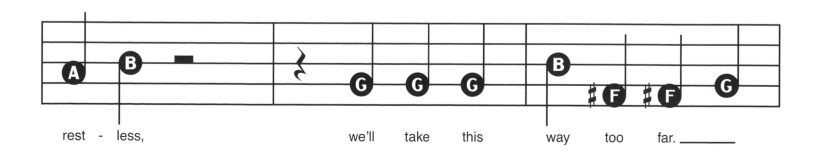

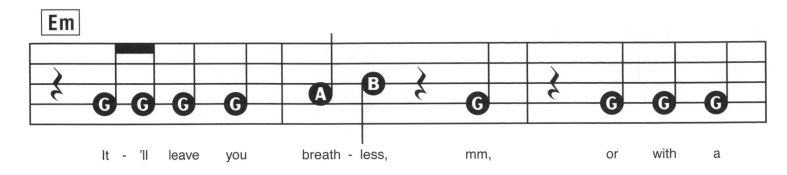

It - 'll leave you breath - less, mm, or with a

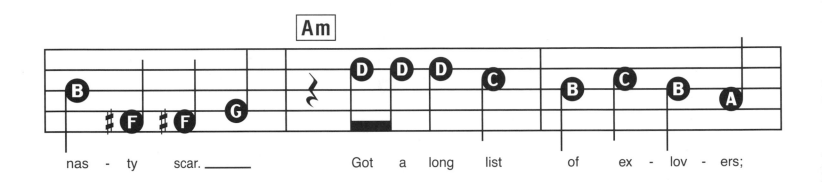

nas - ty scar. _____ Got a long list of ex - lov - ers;

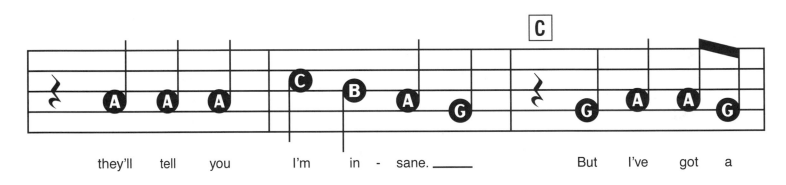

they'll tell you I'm in - sane. _____ But I've got a

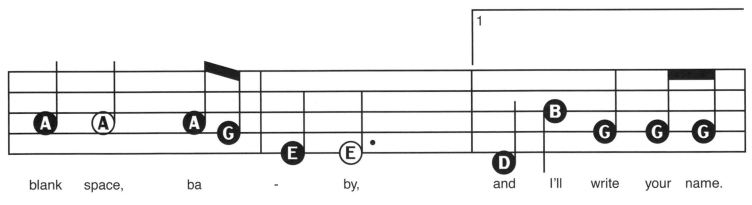

blank space, ba - by, and I'll write your name.

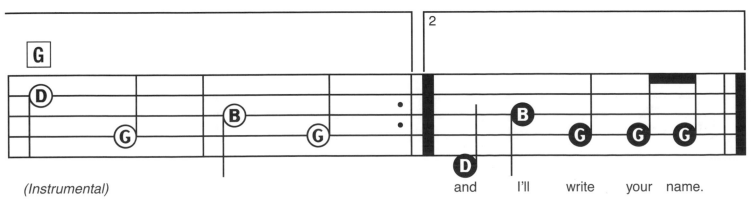

(Instrumental) and I'll write your name.

Dark Horse

Registration 9
Rhythm: Techno or Rock

Words and Music by Katy Perry,
Jordan Houston, Lukasz Gottwald, Sarah Hudson,
Max Martin and Henry Walter

I knew you were, you were gon - na come to me. And
Mark my words, this love will make you lev - i - tate _____

here you are, but you bet - ter choose care - ful - ly, 'cause
like a bird, like a bird with - out a cage. But

I, _____ I'm ca - pa - ble of an - y - thing, _____
down to earth, if you choose to walk a - way, _____

of an - y - thing _____ and ev - 'ry - thing.
don't walk a - way. _____ It's in the

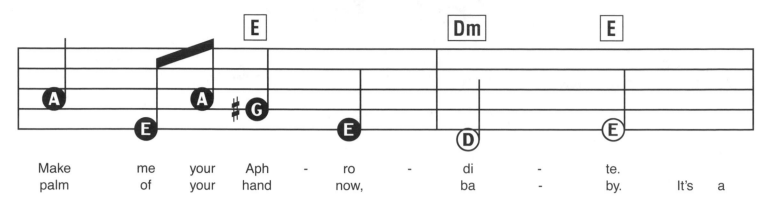

Make me your Aph - ro - di - te.
palm of your hand now, ba - by. It's a

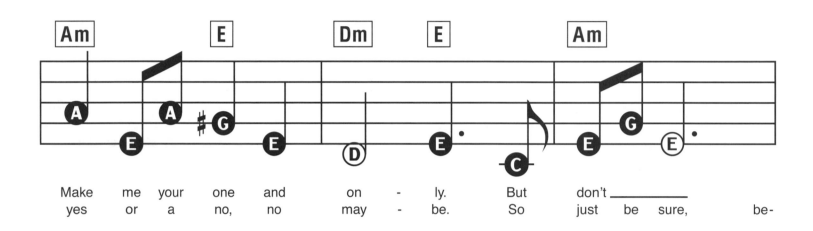

Make me your one and on - ly. But don't _____
yes or a no, no may - be. So just be sure, be-

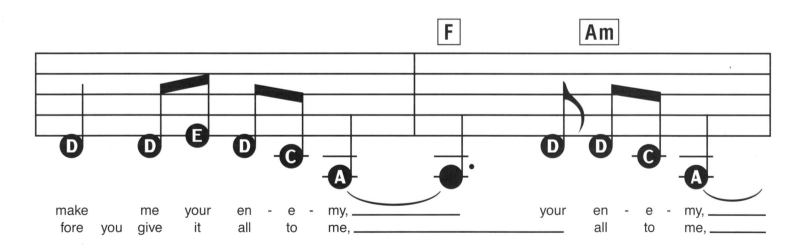

make me your en - e - my, _____ your en - e - my, _____
fore you give it all to me, _____ all to me, _____

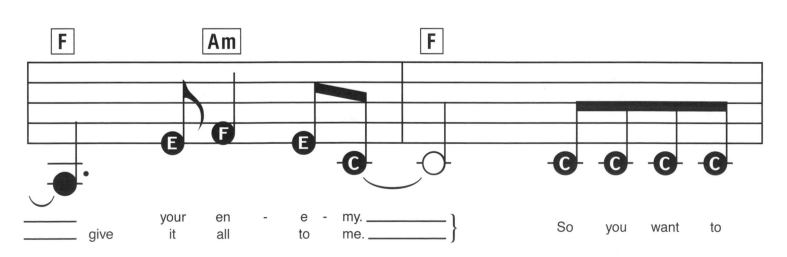

_____ your en - e - my. _____ }
_____ give it all to me. _____

So you want to

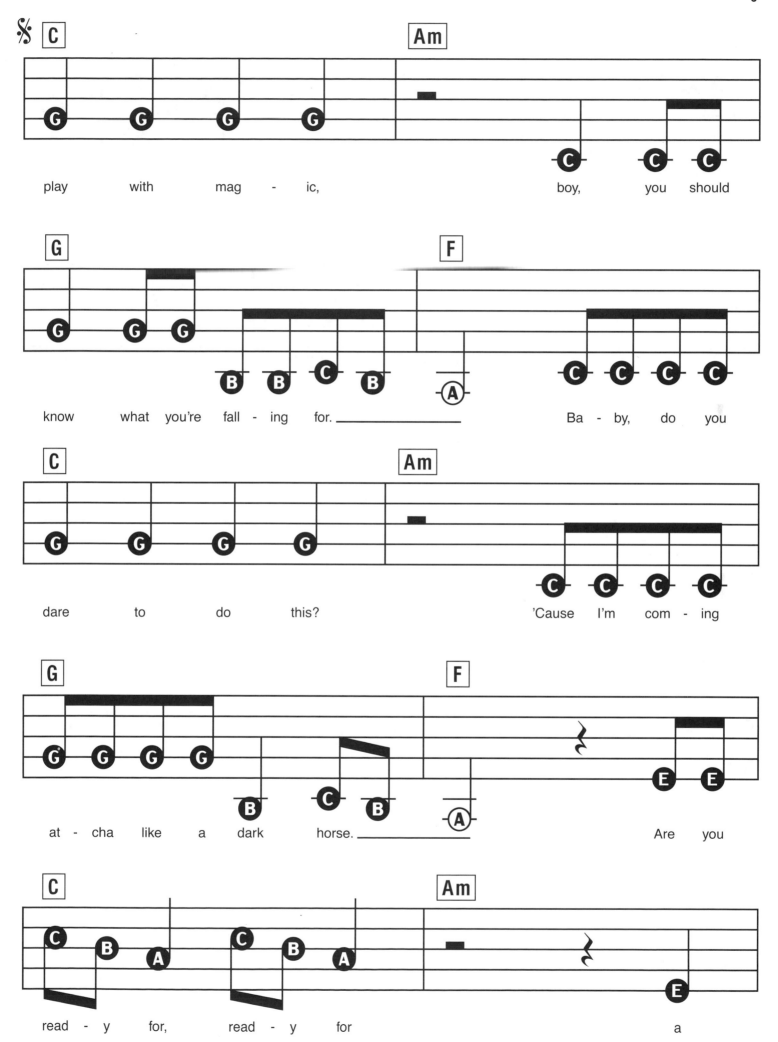

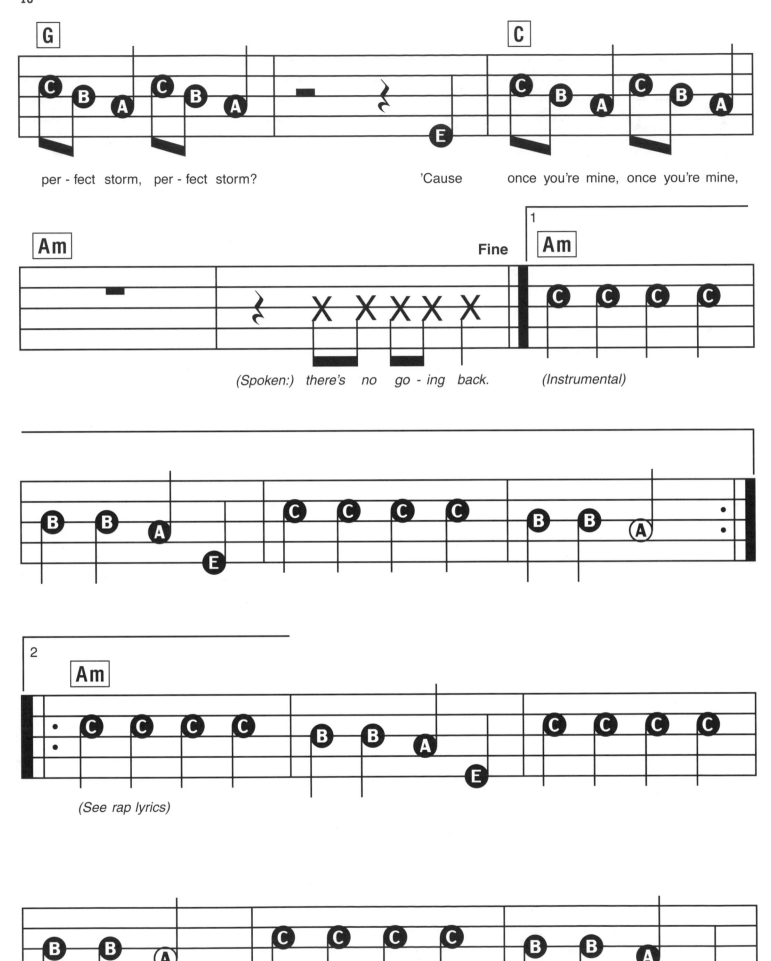

per - fect storm, per - fect storm? 'Cause once you're mine, once you're mine,

(Spoken:) there's no go - ing back. *(Instrumental)*

(See rap lyrics)

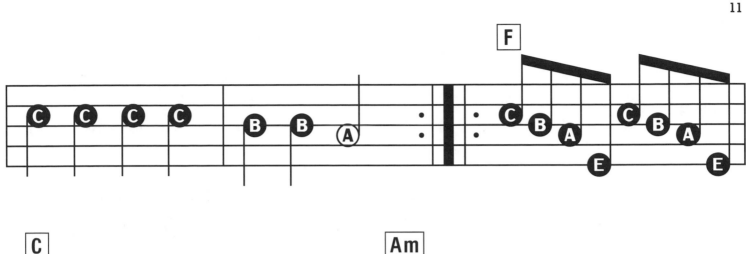

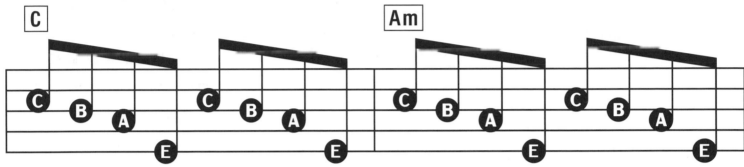

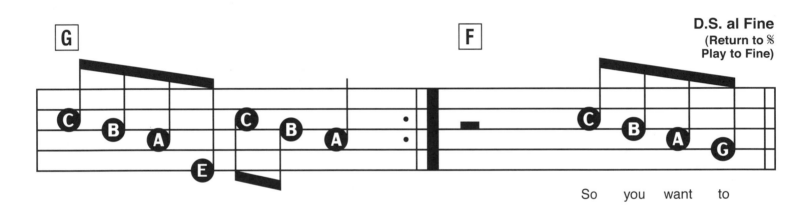

So   you   want   to

Rap lyrics

Uh, she's a beast, I call her Karma,
She'll eat your heart out like Jeffrey Dahmer.
Be careful, try not to lead her on.
Shorty heart is on steroids, 'cause her love is so strong.
You may fall in love when you meet her,
If you get the chance, you better keep her.
She's sweet as pie, but if you break her heart,
She'll turn cold as a freezer.
That fairy tale ending with a knight in shining armor,
She can be my Sleeping Beauty.
I'm gon' put her in a coma.
Now I think I love her,
Shorty so bad, sprung and I don't care
She ride me like a roller coaster,
Turned the bedroom into a fair.
Her love is like a drug,
I was tryna hit it and quit it,
But lil' mama so dope,
I messed around and got addicted.

City of Stars
from LA LA LAND

Registration 8
Rhythm: Ballad

Music by Justin Hurwitz
Lyrics by Benj Pasek & Justin Paul

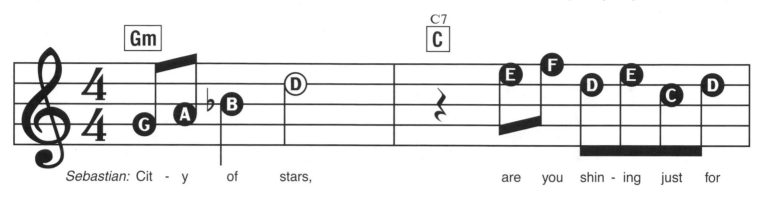

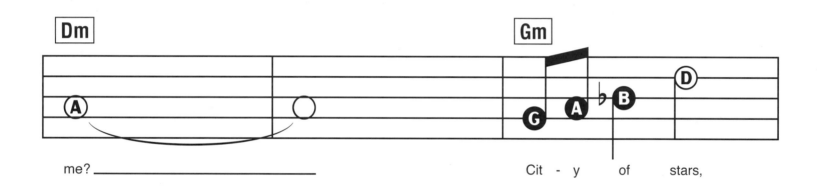

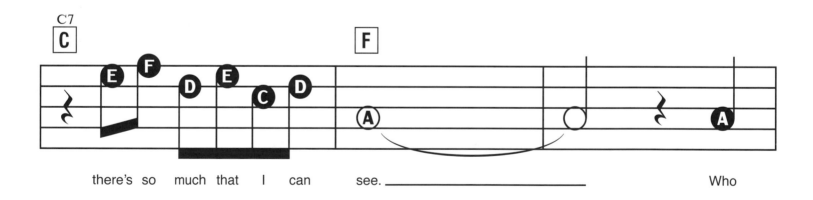

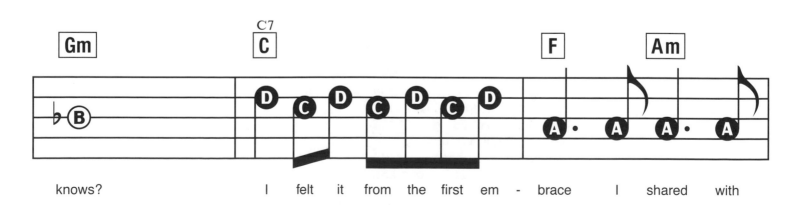

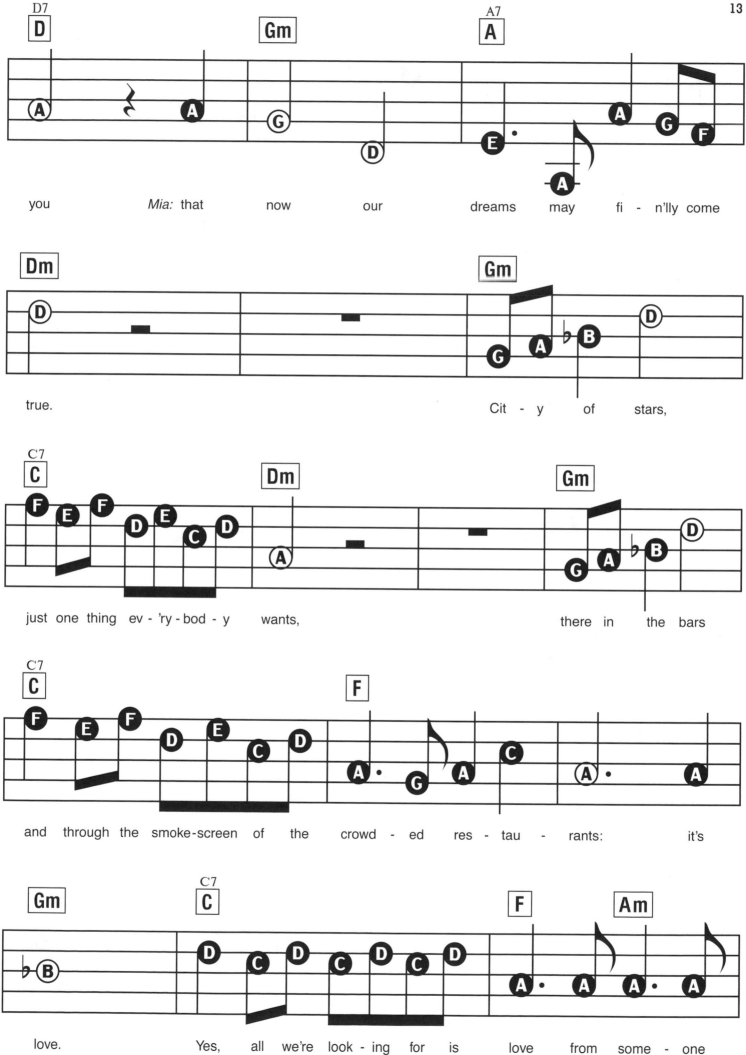

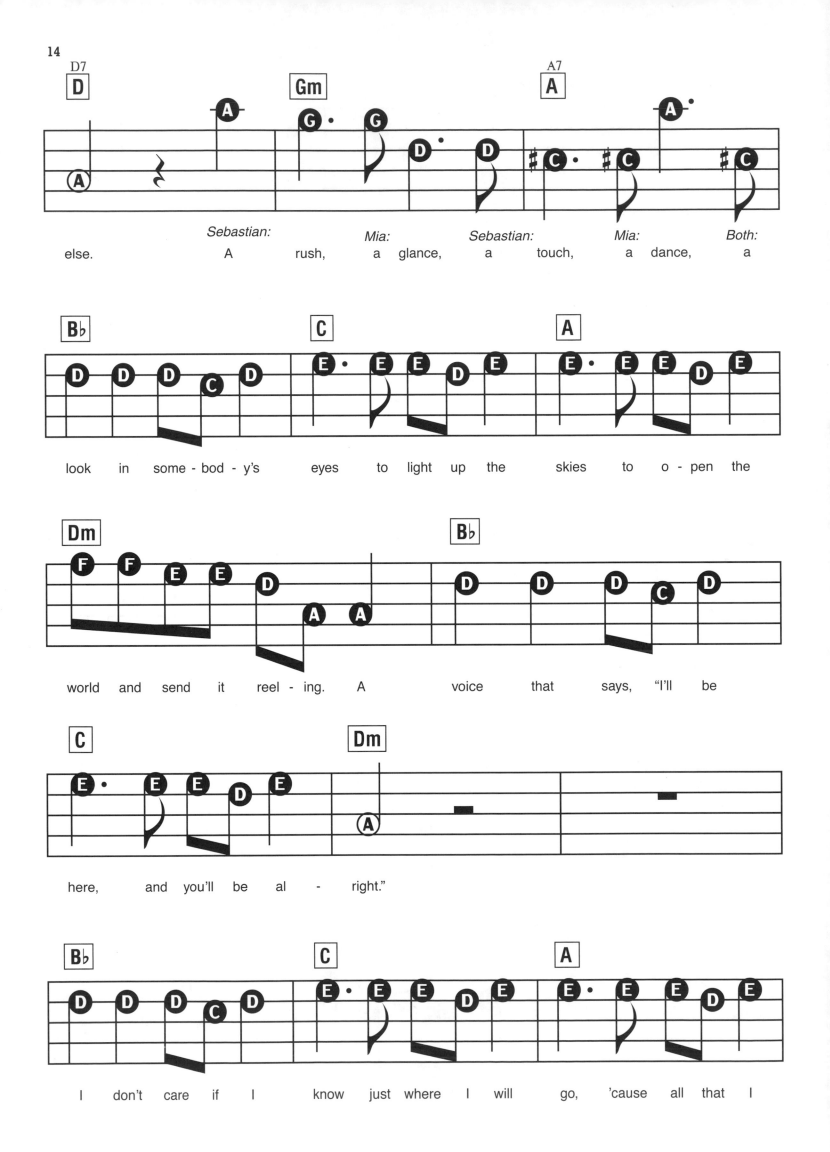

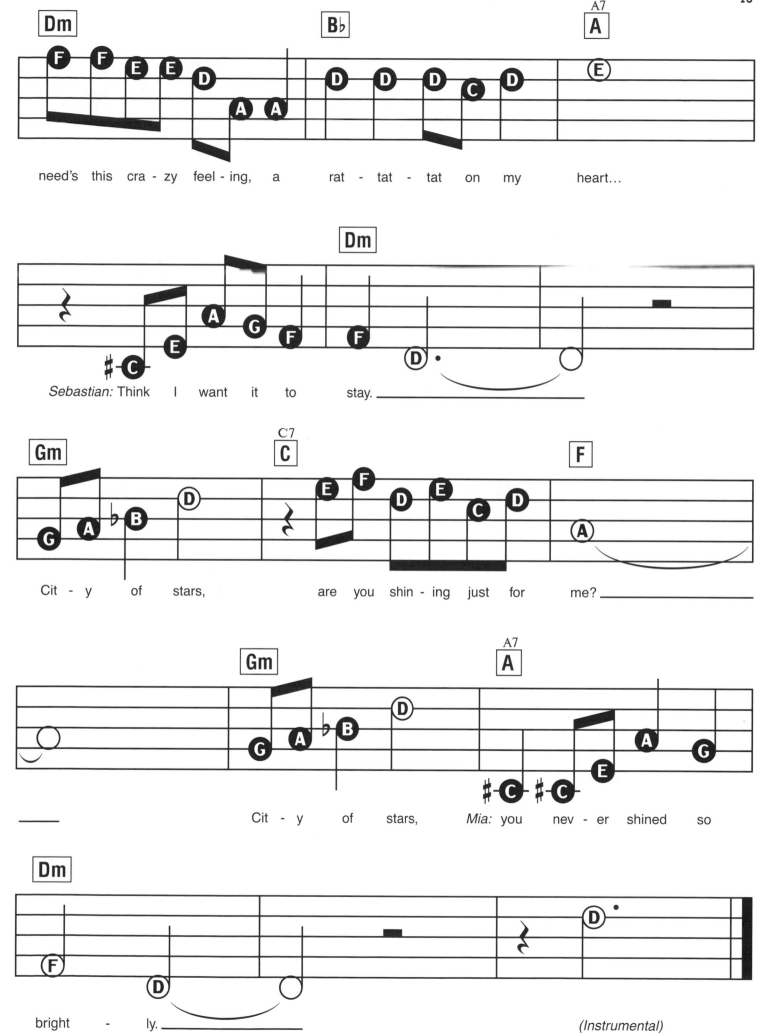

Evermore
from BEAUTY AND THE BEAST

Registration 2
Rhythm: Ballad

Music by Alan Menken
Lyrics by Tim Rice

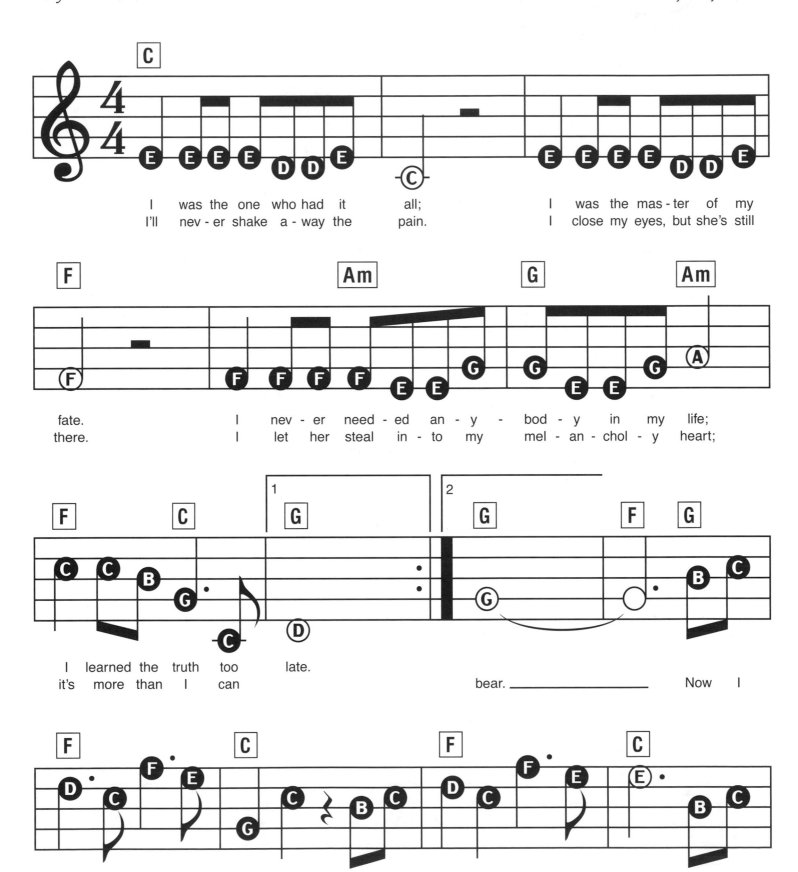

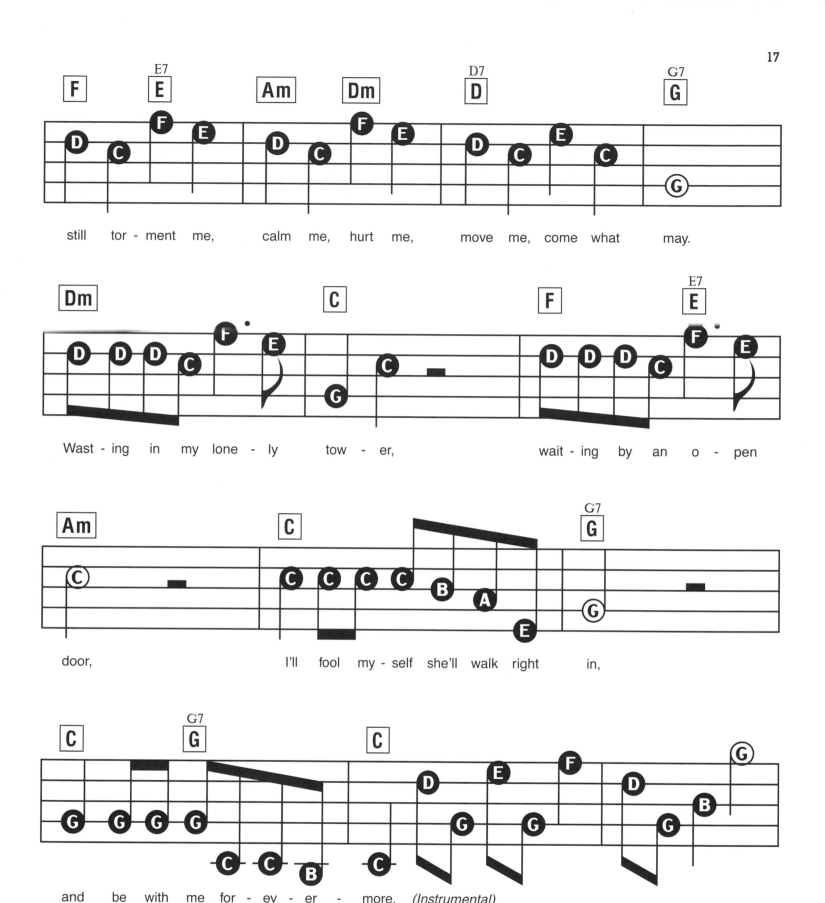

still tor - ment me, calm me, hurt me, move me, come what may.

Wast - ing in my lone - ly tow - er, wait - ing by an o - pen

door, I'll fool my - self she'll walk right in,

and be with me for - ev - er - more. *(Instrumental)*

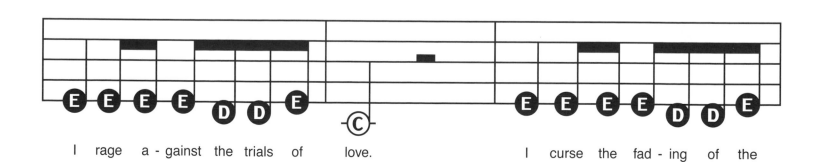

I rage a - gainst the trials of love. I curse the fad - ing of the

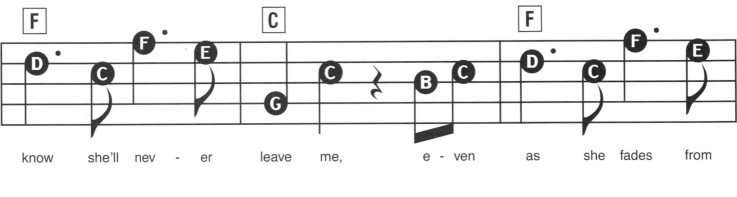

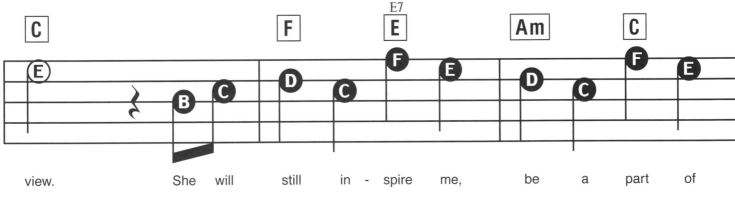

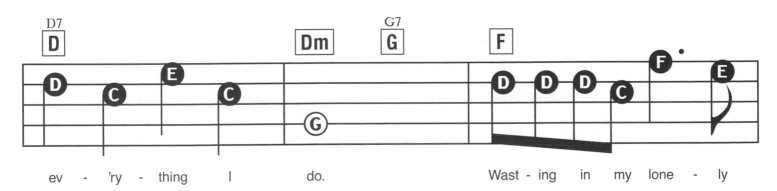

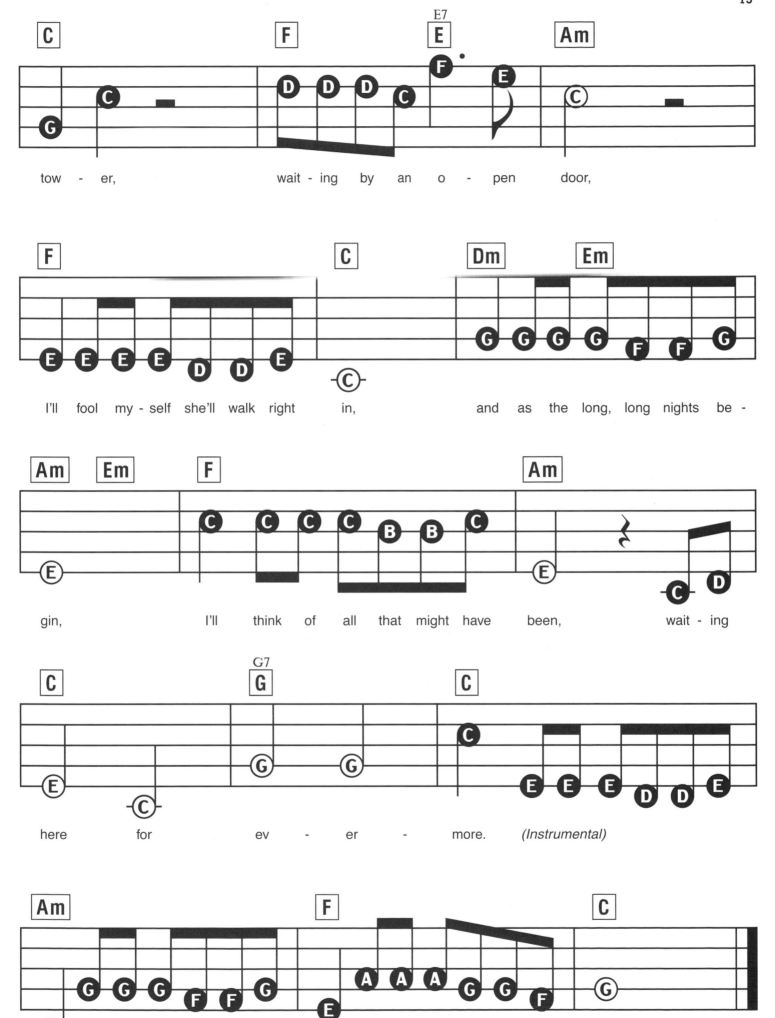

Fight Song

Registration 4
Rhythm: 8-Beat or Rock

Words and Music by Rachel Platten
and Dave Bassett

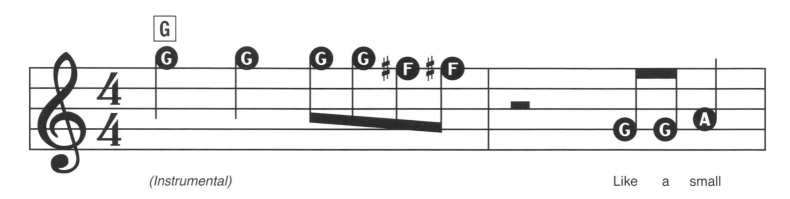

(Instrumental)

Like a small

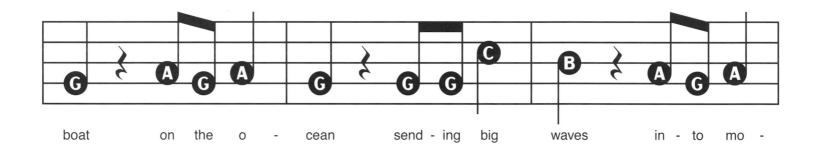

boat   on the o - cean   send - ing big   waves   in - to mo -

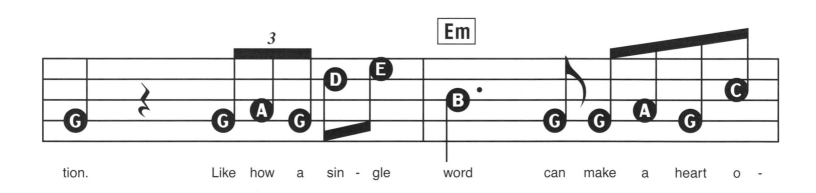

tion.   Like how a sin - gle   word   can make a heart o -

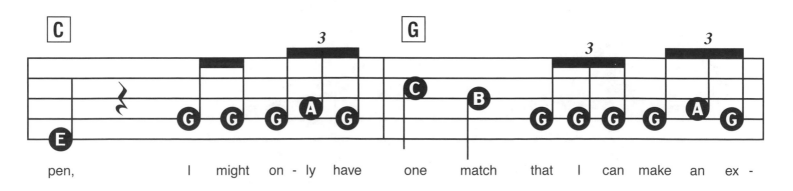

pen,   I might on - ly have   one match that I can make an ex -

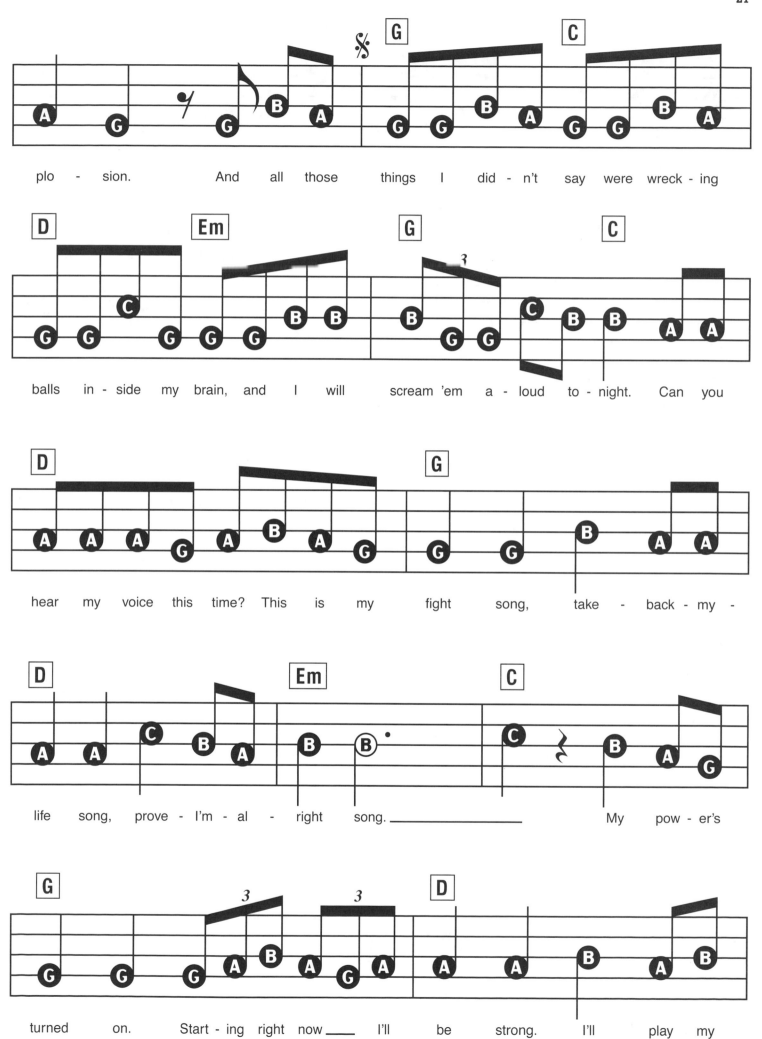

22

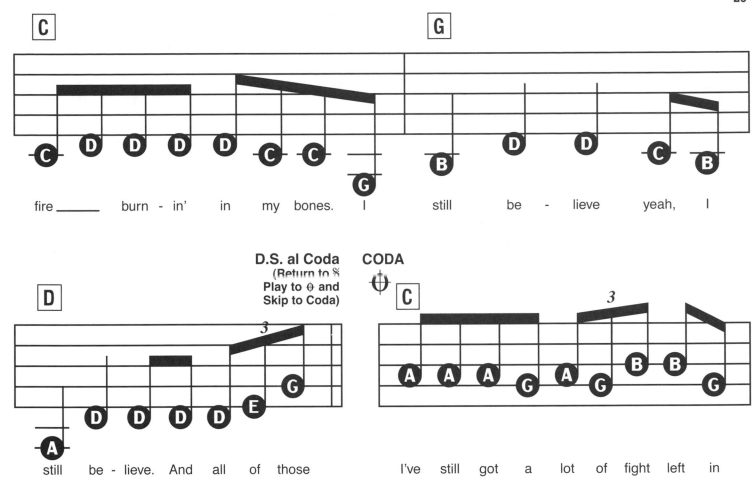

fire _____ burn - in' in my bones. I still be - lieve yeah, I

D.S. al Coda
(Return to %
Play to ϕ and
Skip to Coda)

CODA

still be - lieve. And all of those

I've still got a lot of fight left in

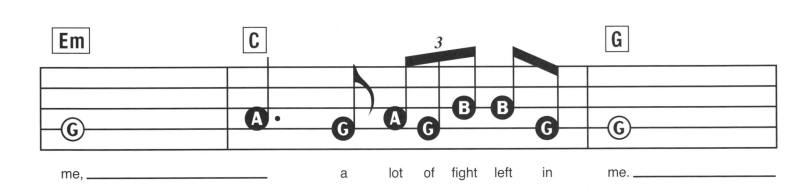

me, _____ a lot of fight left in me. _____

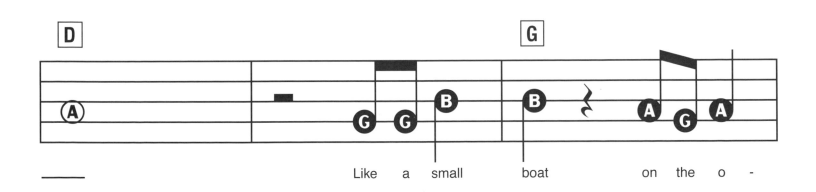

_____ Like a small boat on the o -

24

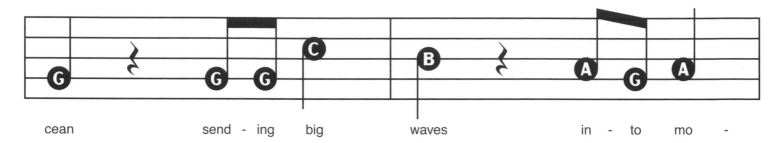

cean   send - ing   big   waves   in - to   mo -

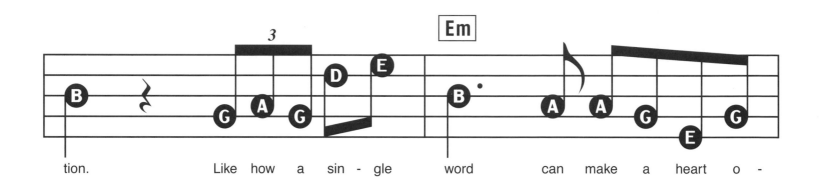

tion.   Like   how   a   sin - gle   word   can   make   a   heart   o -

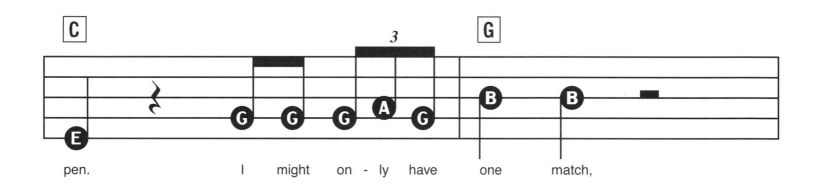

pen.   I   might   on - ly   have   one   match,

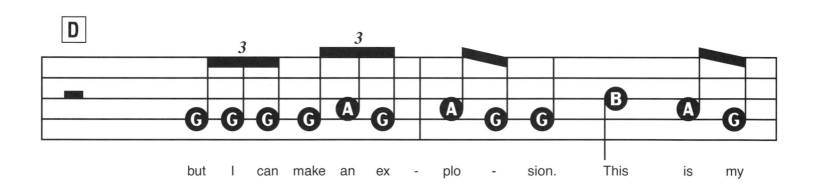

but   I   can   make   an   ex - plo - sion.   This   is   my

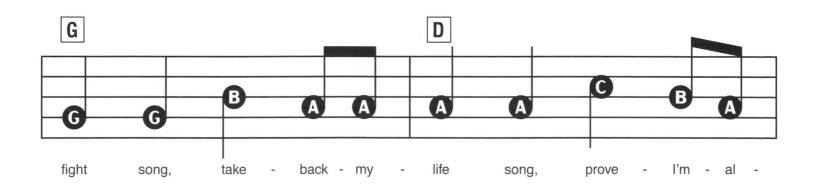

fight   song,   take - back - my - life   song,   prove - I'm - al -

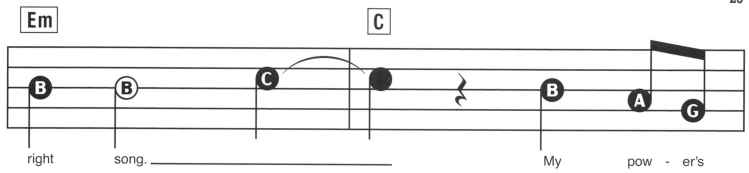

right song. _____ My pow - er's

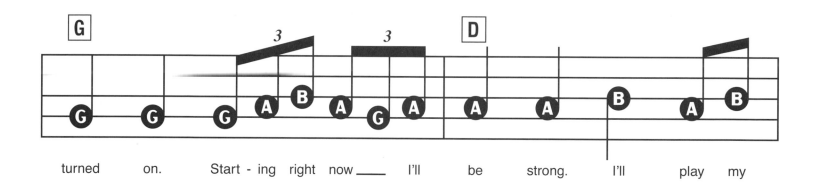

turned on. Start - ing right now ____ I'll be strong. I'll play my

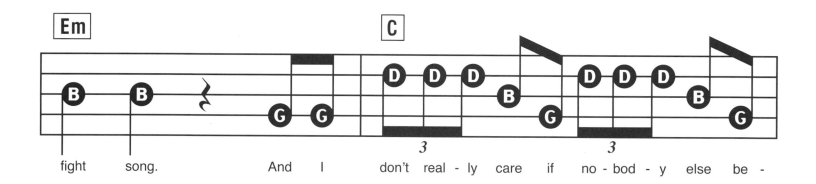

fight song. And I don't real - ly care if no - bod - y else be -

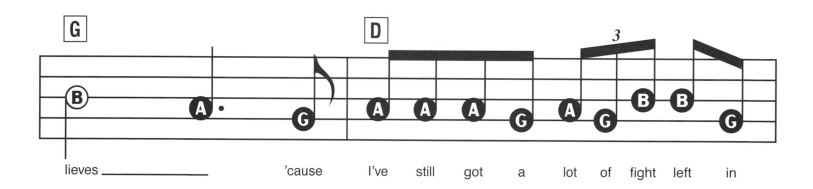

lieves _____ 'cause I've still got a lot of fight left in

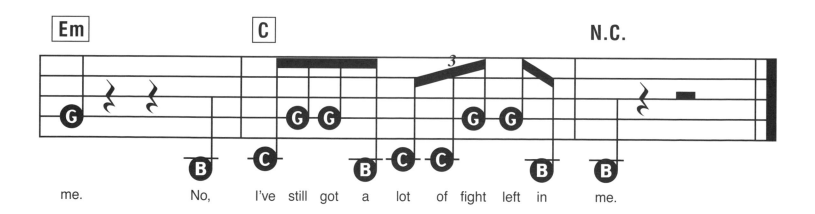

me. No, I've still got a lot of fight left in me.

H.O.L.Y.

Registration 8
Rhythm: Ballad or Rock

Words and Music by busbee,
Nate Cyphert and William Wiik Larsen

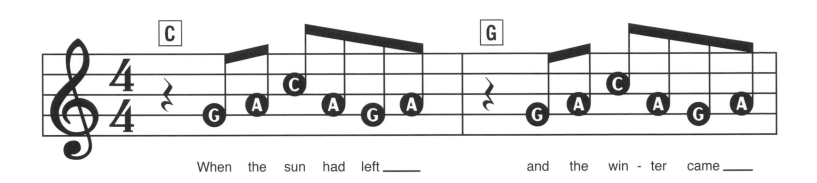

When the sun had left _____ and the win - ter came _____

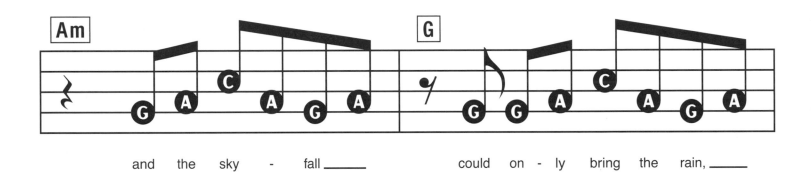

and the sky - fall _____ could on - ly bring the rain, _____

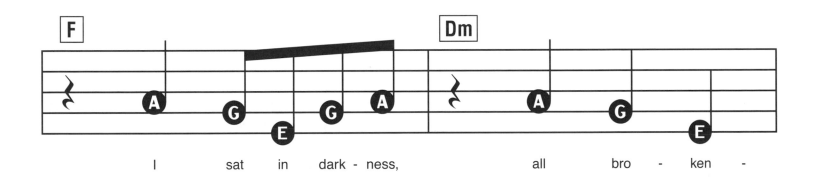

I sat in dark - ness, all bro - ken -

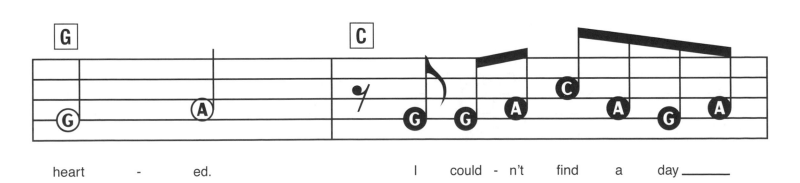

heart - ed. I could - n't find a day _____

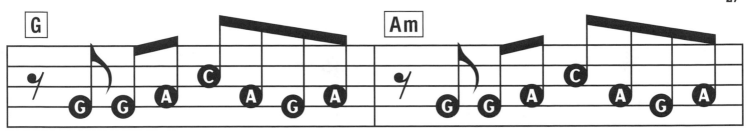

I did - n't feel a - lone. _____ I nev - er meant to cry, _____

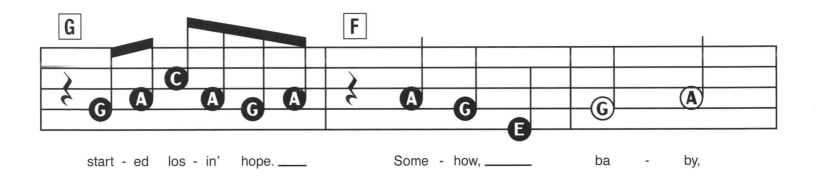

start - ed los - in' hope. ____ Some - how, _____ ba - by,

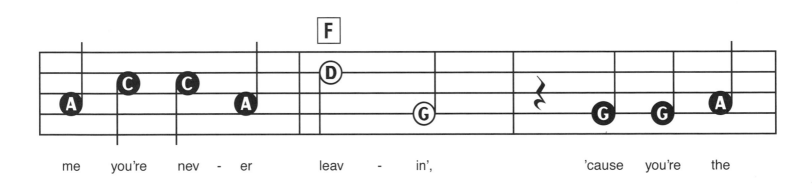

you broke through and saved me. You're an an - gel. Tell

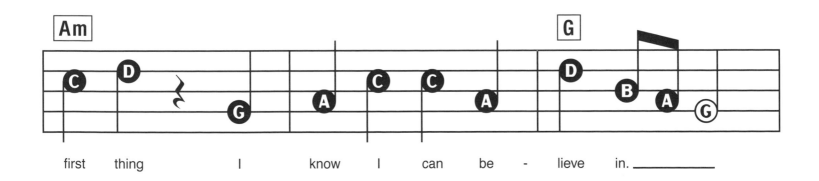

me you're nev - er leav - in', 'cause you're the

first thing I know I can be - lieve in. _____

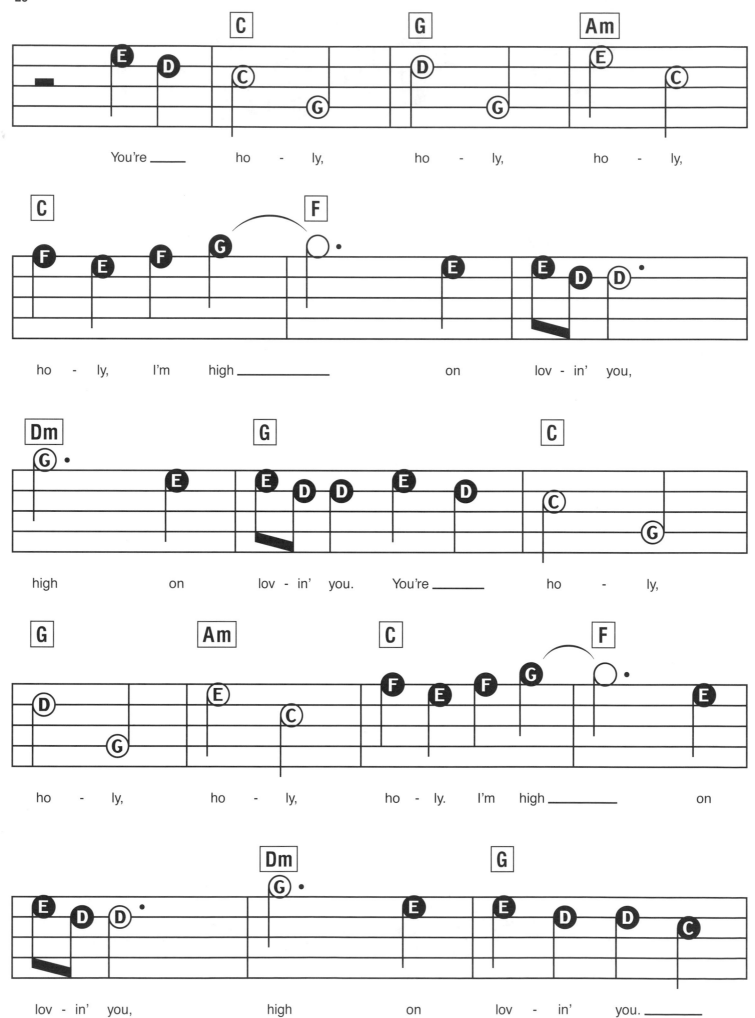

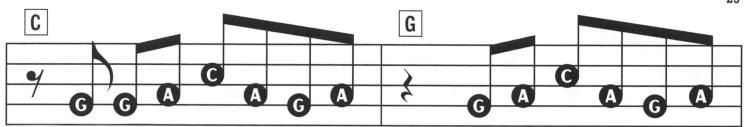

You made the bright - est days _____ from the dark - est nights. _____

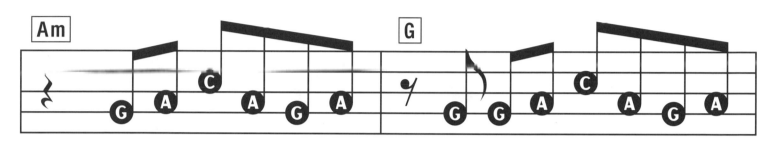

You're the riv - er bank _____ where I was bap - tized, _____

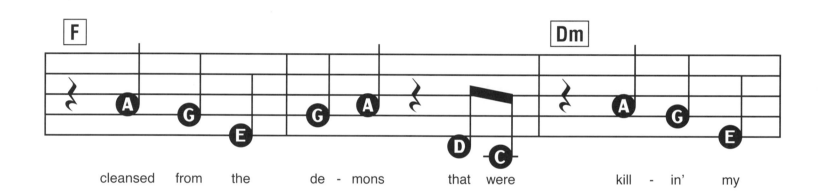

cleansed from the de - mons that were kill - in' my

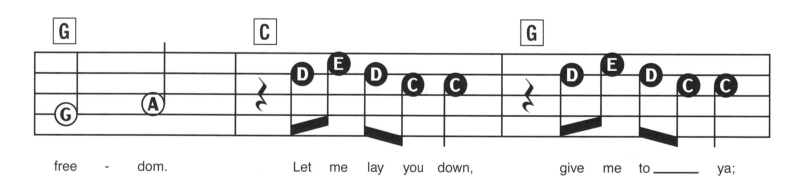

free - dom. Let me lay you down, give me to _____ ya;

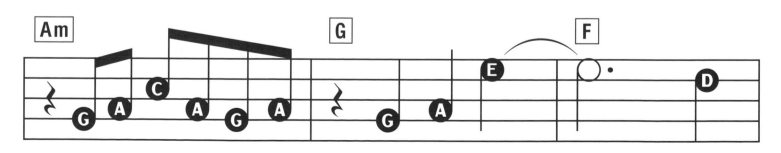

get you sing - in', babe, _____ hal - le - lu - jah. _____

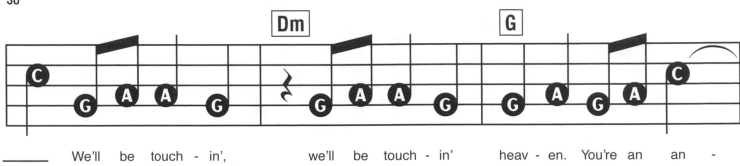

We'll be touch - in', we'll be touch - in' heav - en. You're an an -

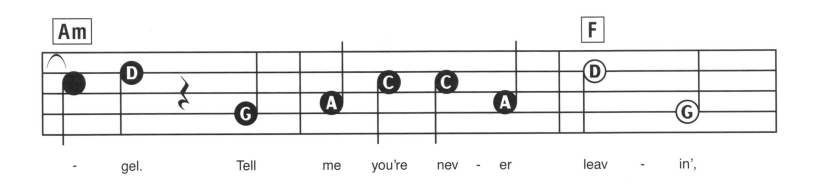

- gel. Tell me you're nev - er leav - in',

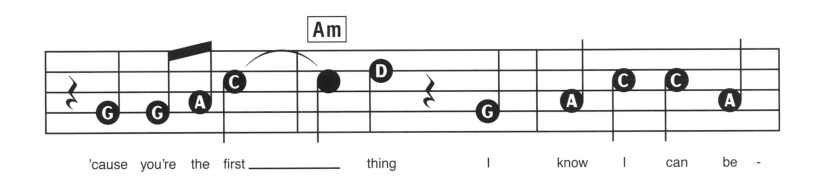

'cause you're the first _____ thing I know I can be -

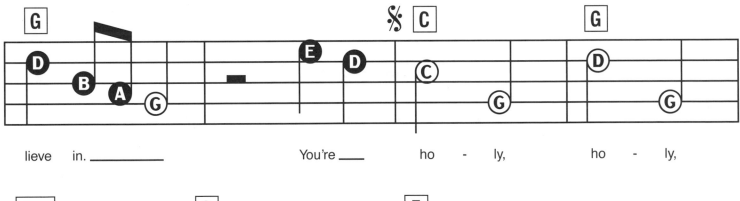

lieve in. _____ You're ___ ho - ly, ho - ly,

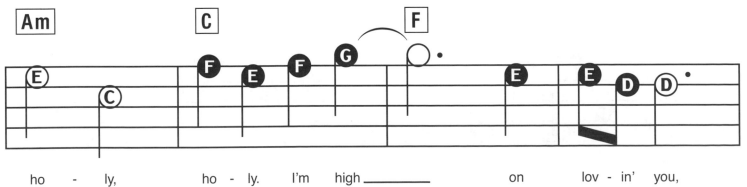

ho - ly, ho - ly. I'm high _____ on lov - in' you,

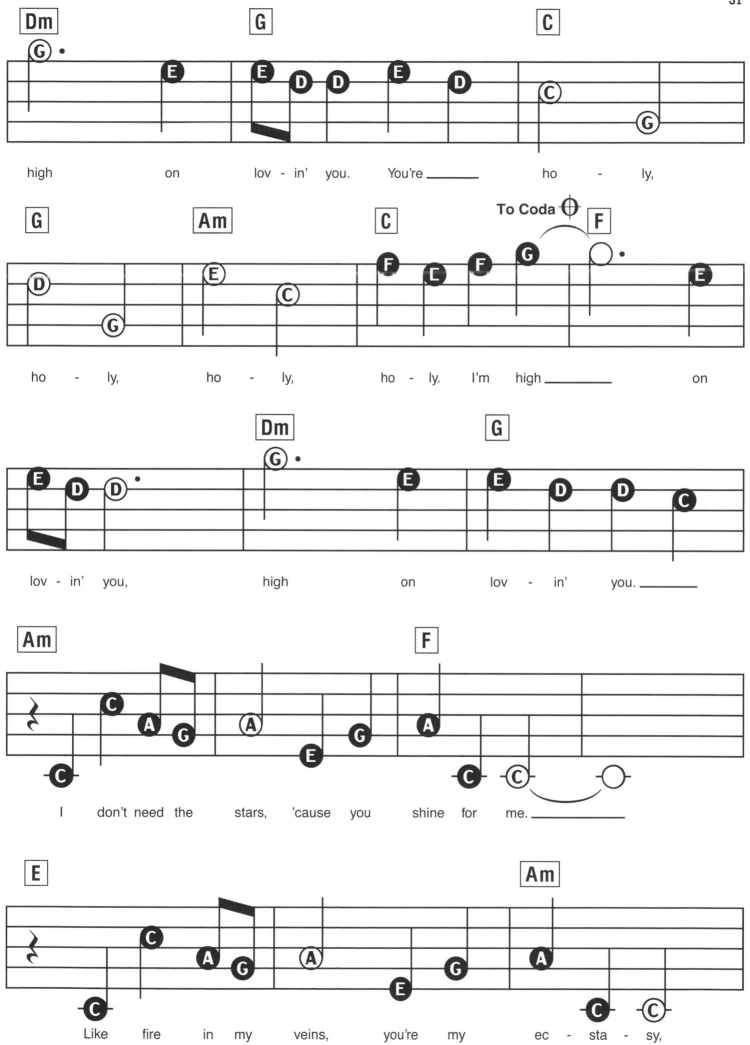

D.S. al Coda
(Return to %
Play to ⊕ and
Skip to Coda)

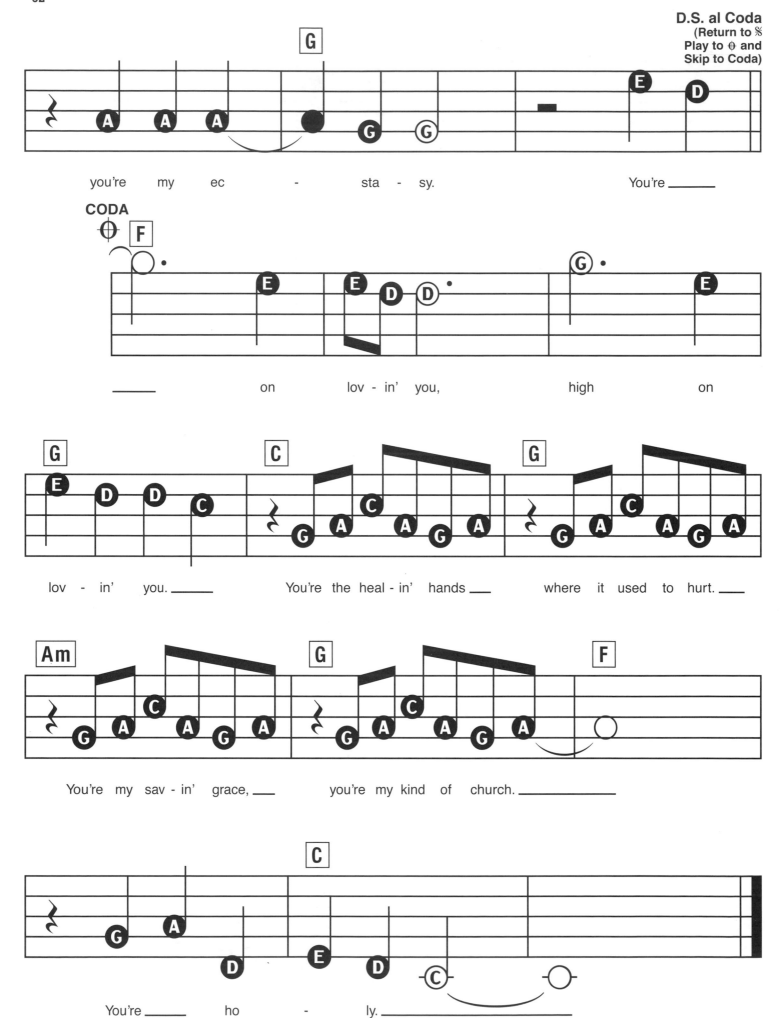

you're my ec - sta - sy. You're _____

CODA

_____ on lov - in' you, high on

lov - in' you. _____ You're the heal - in' hands ___ where it used to hurt. ___

You're my sav - in' grace, ___ you're my kind of church. _____

You're _____ ho - ly. _____

How Far I'll Go
from MOANA

Registration 1
Rhythm: Pop or Techno

Music and Lyrics by
Lin-Manuel Miranda

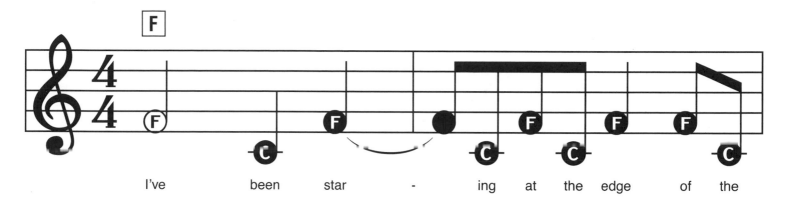

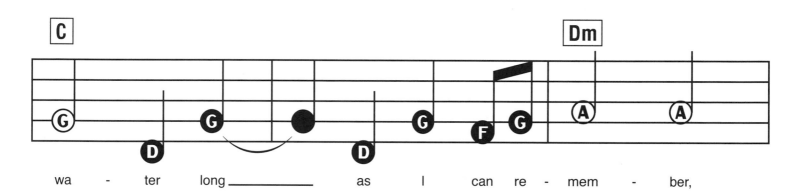

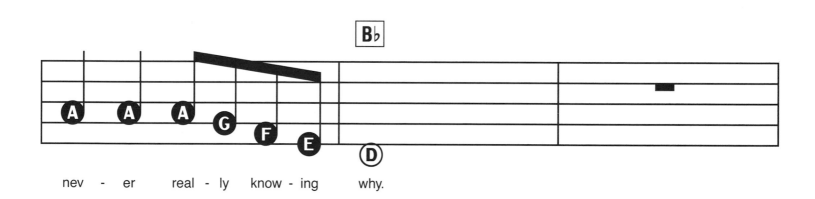

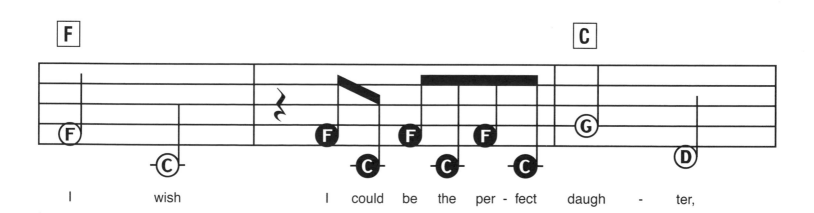

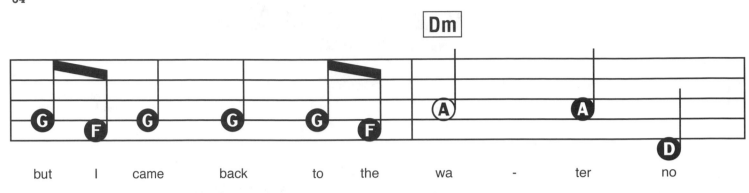

but I came back to the wa - ter no

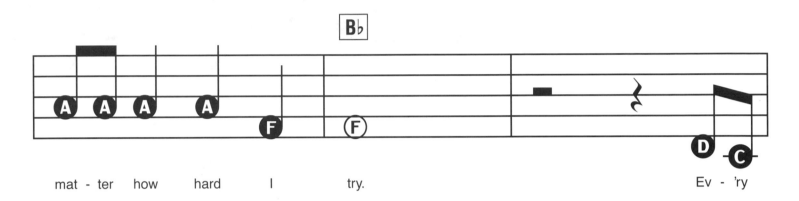

mat - ter how hard I try. Ev - 'ry

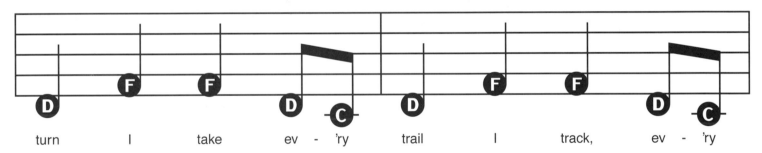

turn I take ev - 'ry trail I track, ev - 'ry

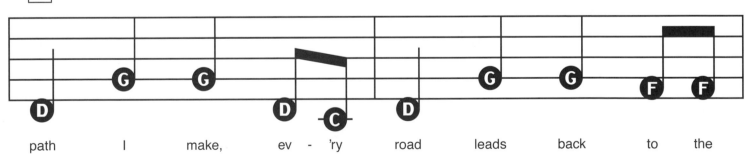

path I make, ev - 'ry road leads back to the

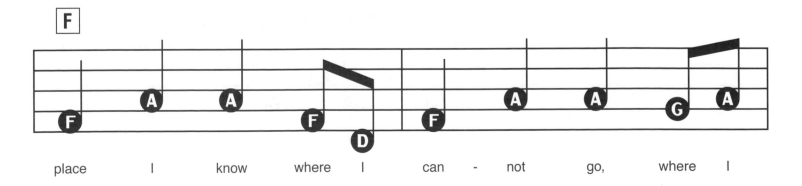

place I know where I can - not go, where I

35

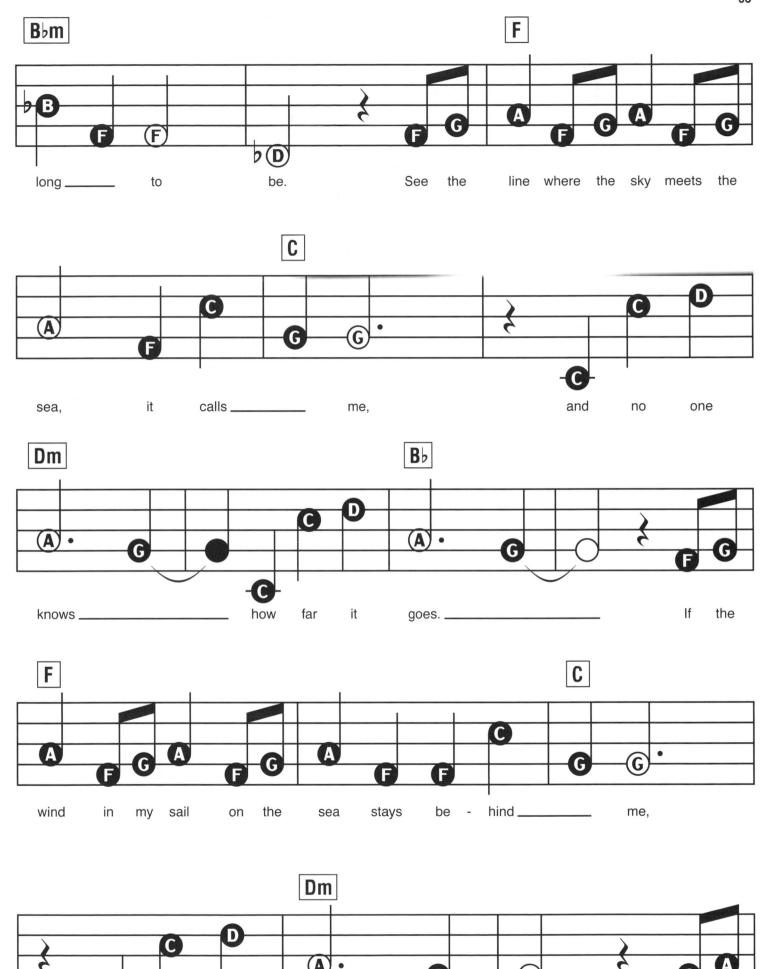

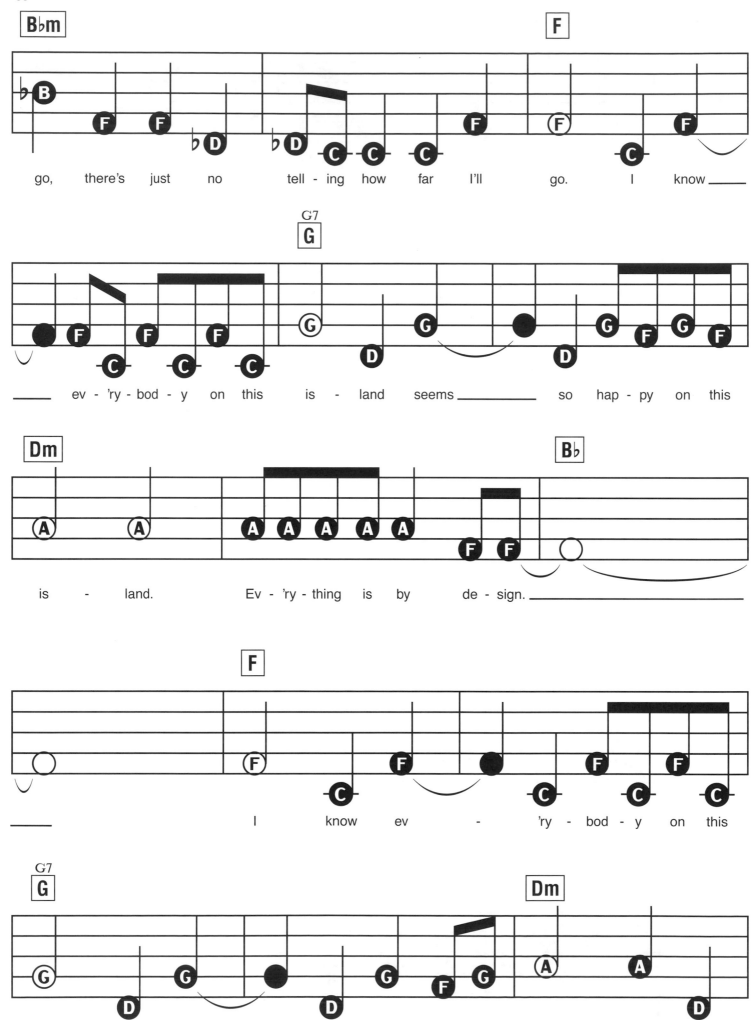

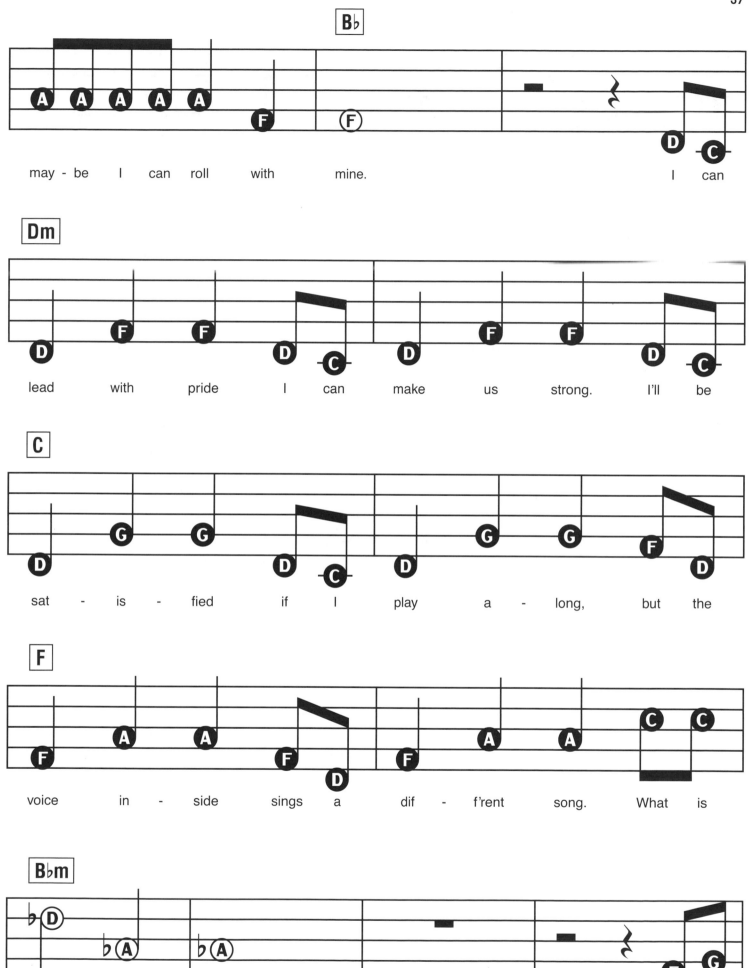

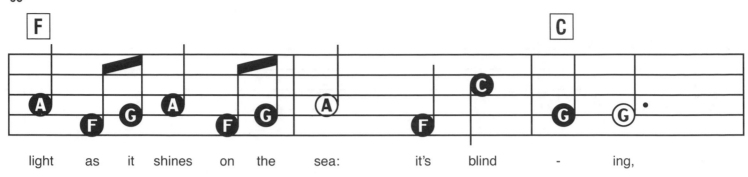

light as it shines on the sea: it's blind - ing,

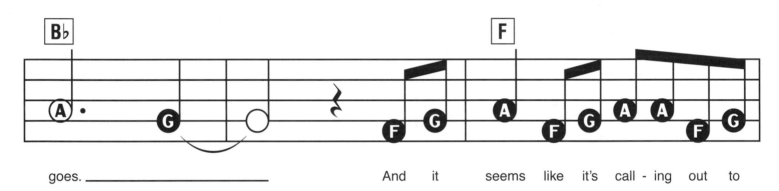

but no one knows _____ how deep it

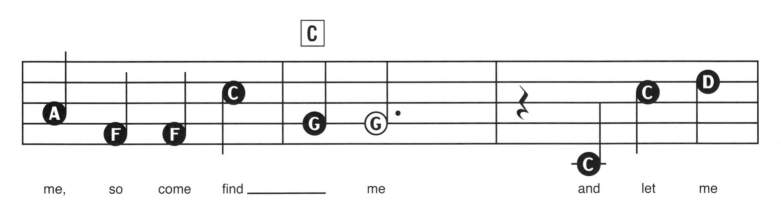

goes. _____ And it seems like it's call - ing out to

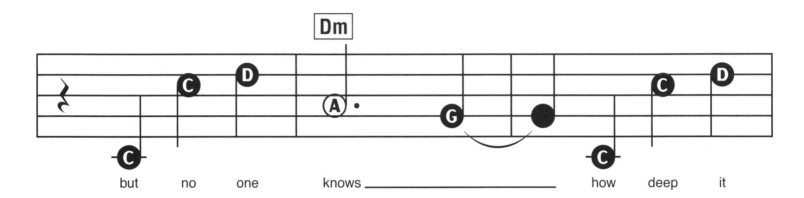

me, so come find _____ me and let me

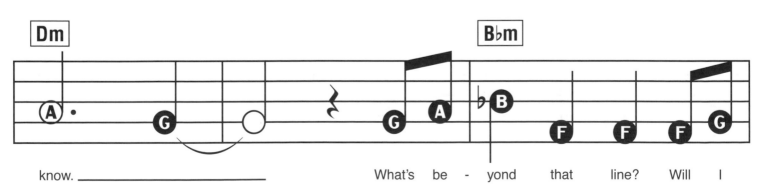

know. _____ What's be - yond that line? Will I

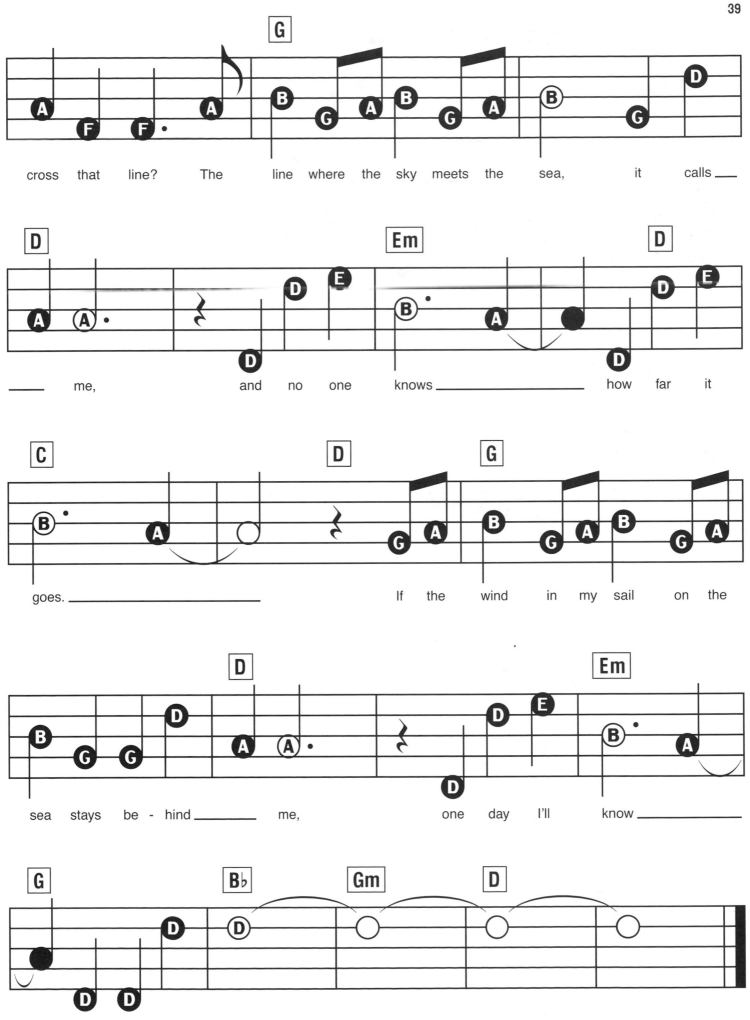

I'm Not the Only One

Registration 8
Rhythm: 8-Beat or Rock

Words and Music by Sam Smith
and James Napier

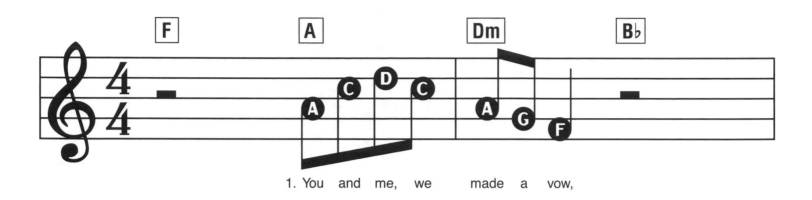

1. You and me, we made a vow,

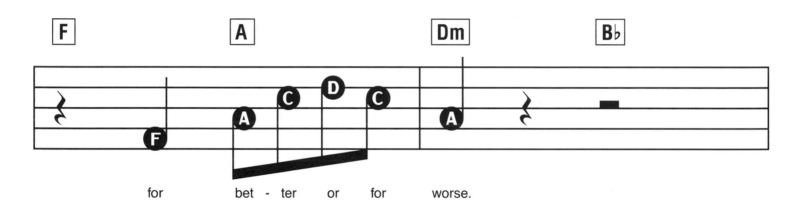

for bet - ter or for worse.

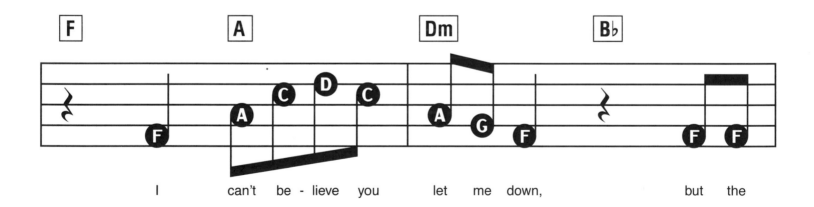

I can't be - lieve you let me down, but the

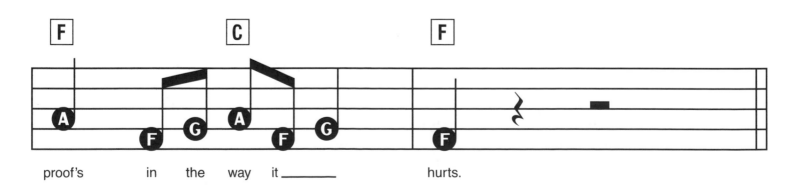

proof's in the way it _____ hurts.

42

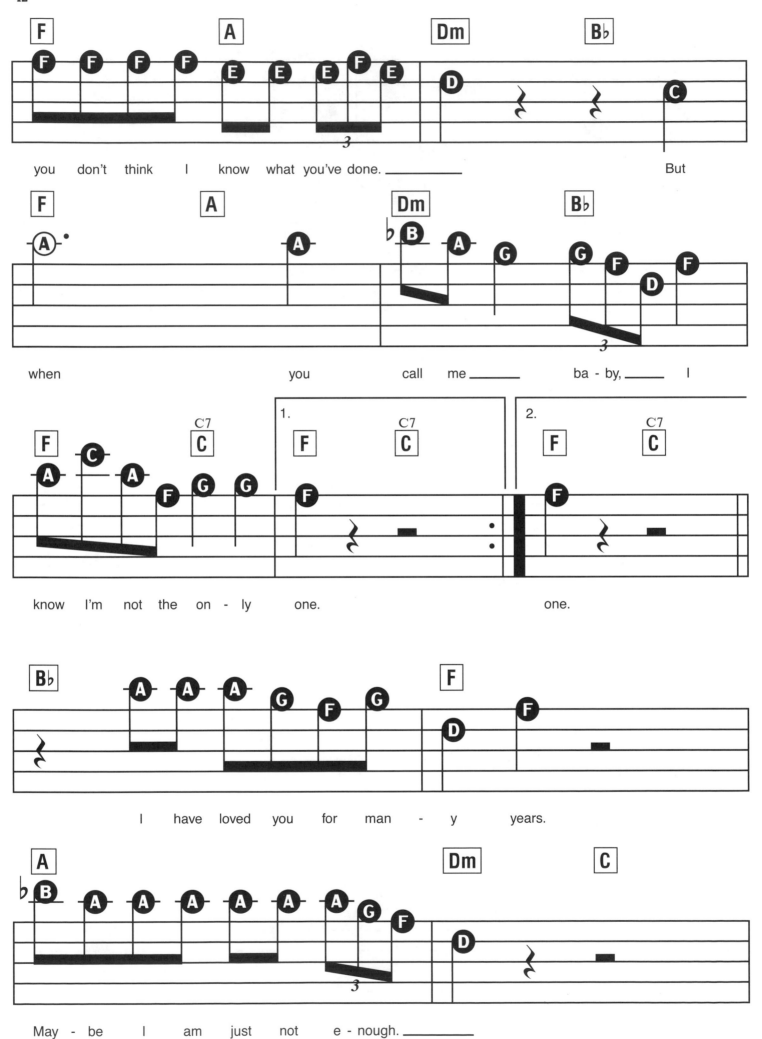

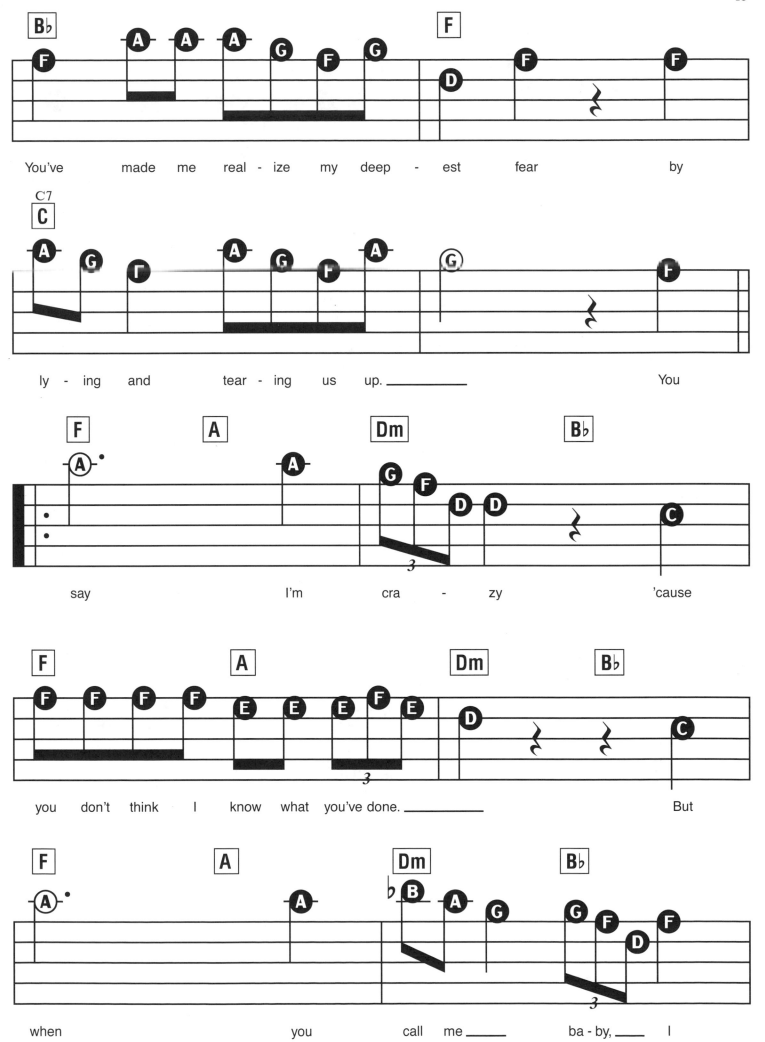

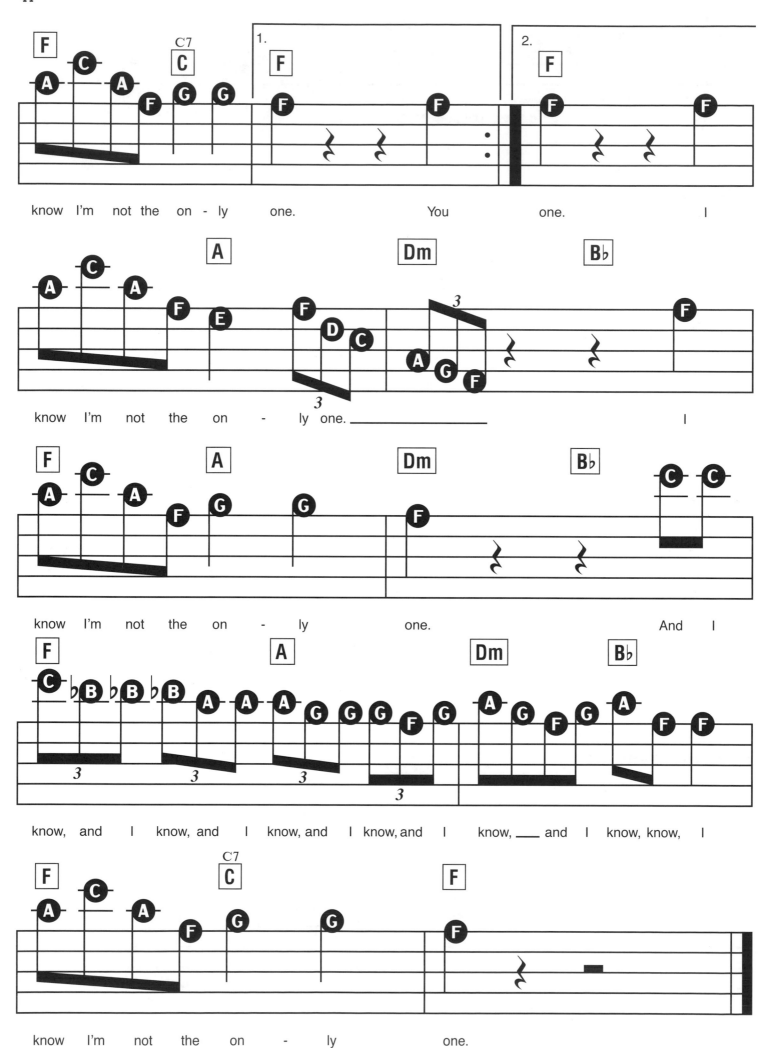

Look What You Made Me Do

Registration 3
Rhythm: Pop or Rock

Words and Music by Taylor Swift,
Jack Antonoff, Richard Fairbrass,
Fred Fairbrass and Rob Manzoli

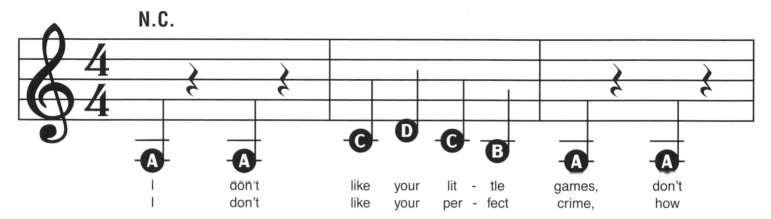

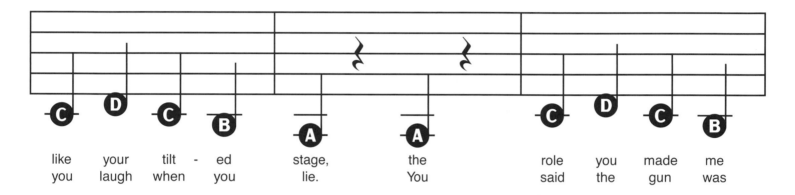

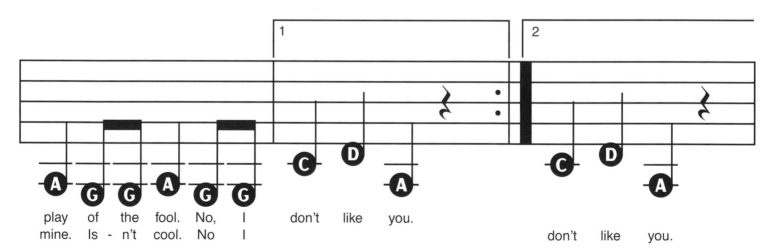

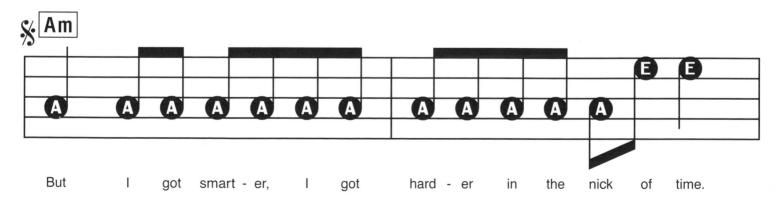

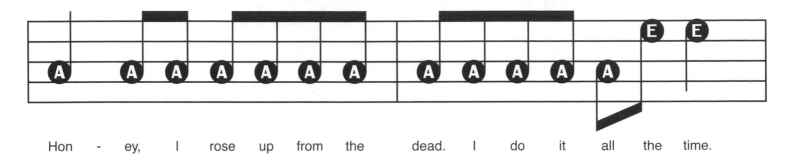

Hon - ey, I rose up from the dead. I do it all the time.

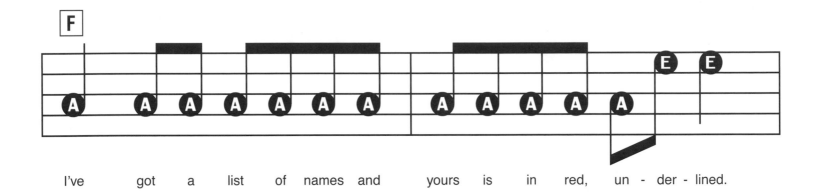

F

I've got a list of names and yours is in red, un - der - lined.

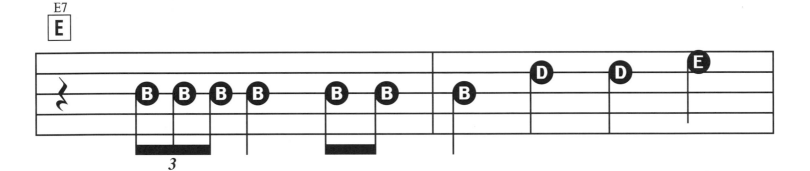

E7
E

3

I check it once, then I check it twice, oh!

Am

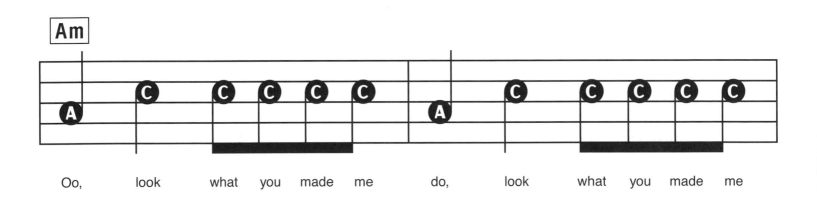

Oo, look what you made me do, look what you made me

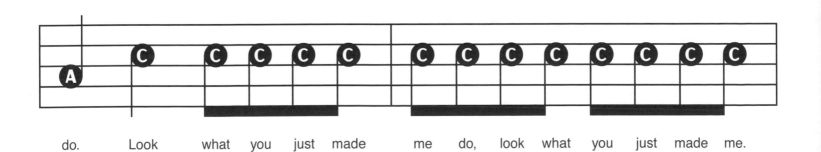

do. Look what you just made me do, look what you just made me.

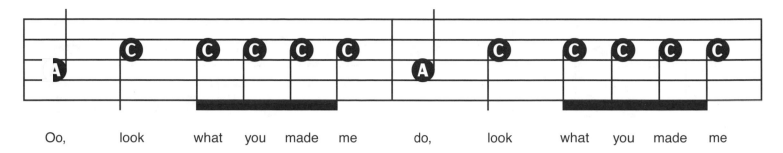

Oo, look what you made me do, look what you made me

To Coda ⊕

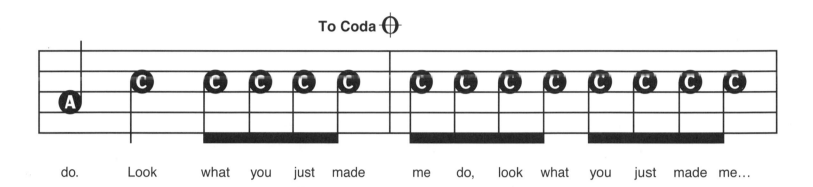

do. Look what you just made me do, look what you just made me…

N.C.

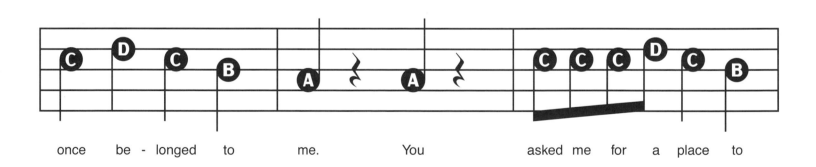

I don't like your king - dom keys; they

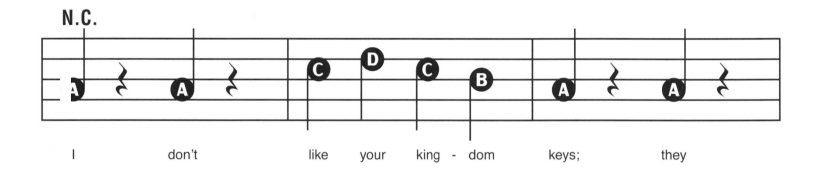

once be - longed to me. You asked me for a place to

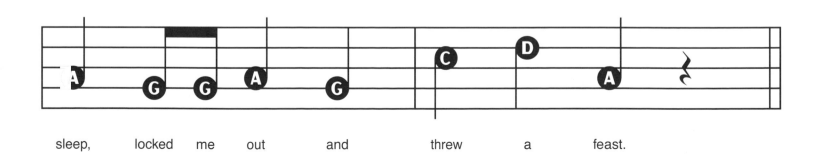

sleep, locked me out and threw a feast.

48

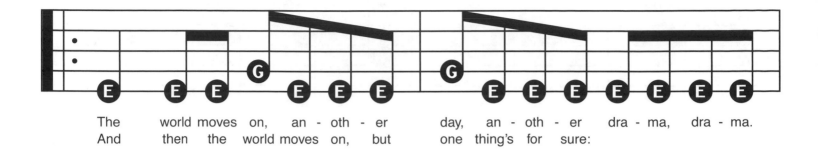

The world moves on, an - oth - er day, an - oth - er dra - ma, dra - ma.
And then the world moves on, but one thing's for sure:

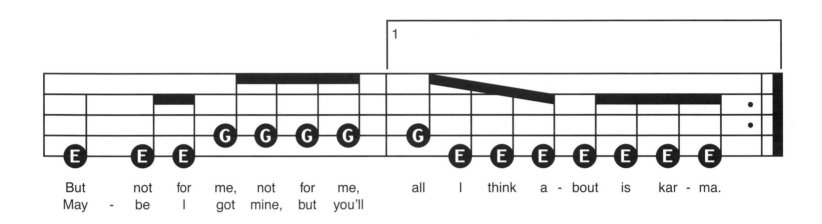

But not for me, not for me, all I think a - bout is kar - ma.
May - be I got mine, but you'll

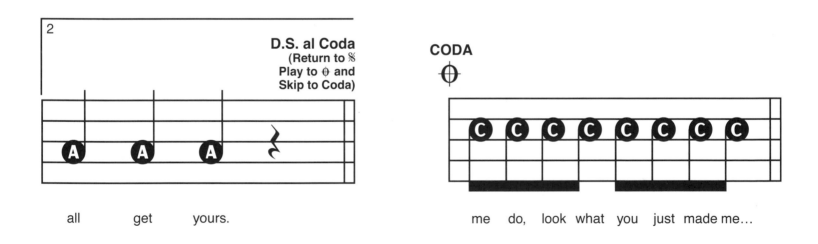

D.S. al Coda
(Return to ℅
Play to ⊕ and
Skip to Coda)

all get yours.

CODA

me do, look what you just made me…

Am

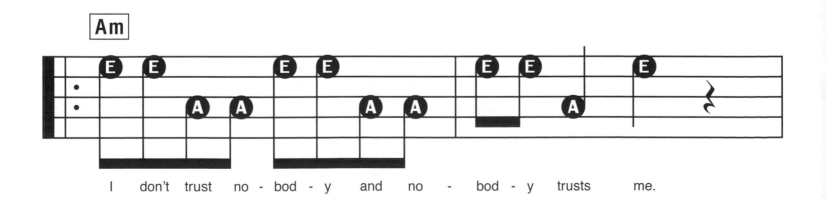

I don't trust no - bod - y and no - bod - y trusts me.

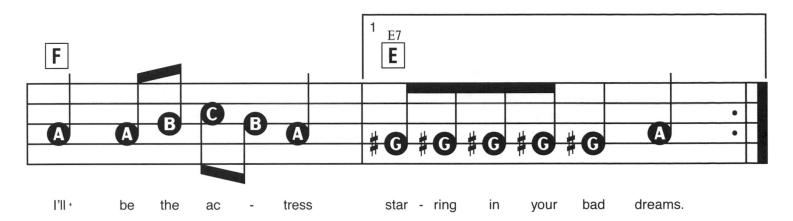

I'll be the ac - tress star - ring in your bad dreams.

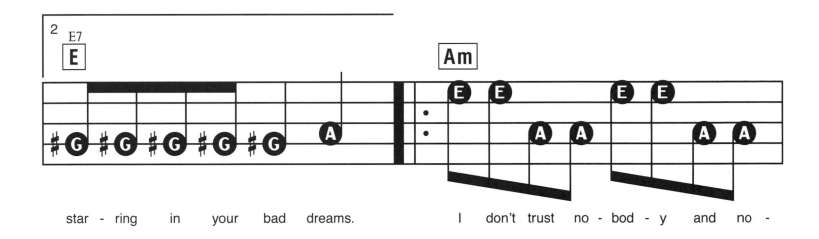

star - ring in your bad dreams. I don't trust no - bod - y and no -

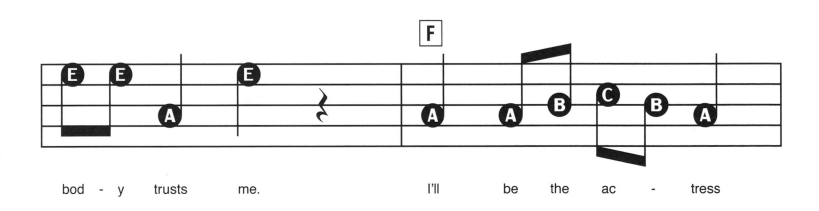

bod - y trusts me. I'll be the ac - tress

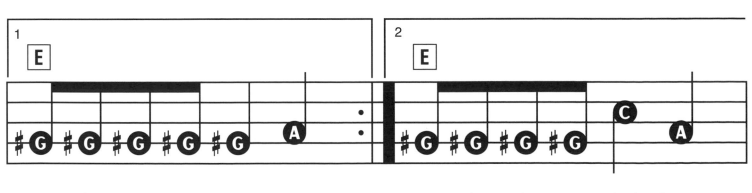

star - ring in your bad dreams.   star - ring in your bad dreams.

Am

(Instrumental)

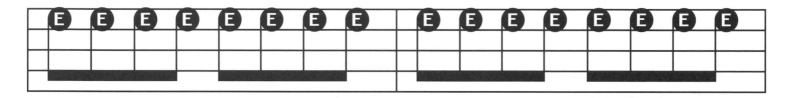

(Spoken:) "I'm sorry, the old Taylor

F

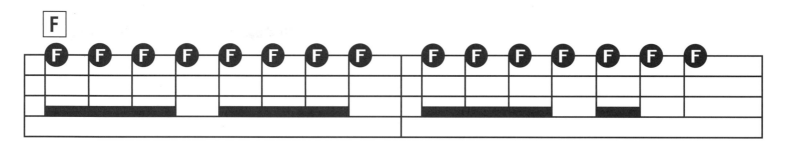

can't come to the phone right   *Why?*

E7

E   **N.C.**

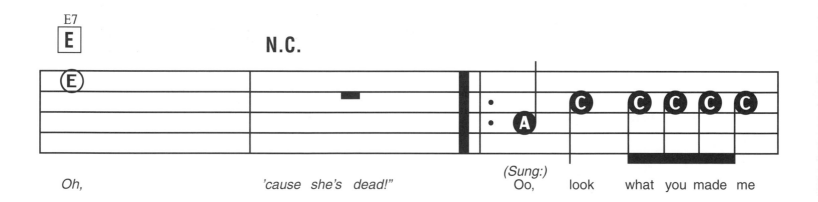

Oh,   *'cause she's dead!"*   *(Sung:)* Oo,   look   what you made me

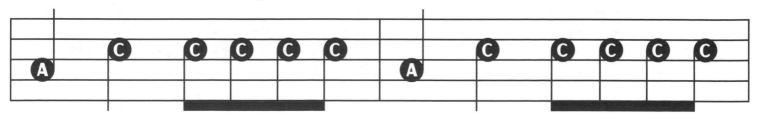

do,   look   what   you made me   do.   Look   what   you   just   made

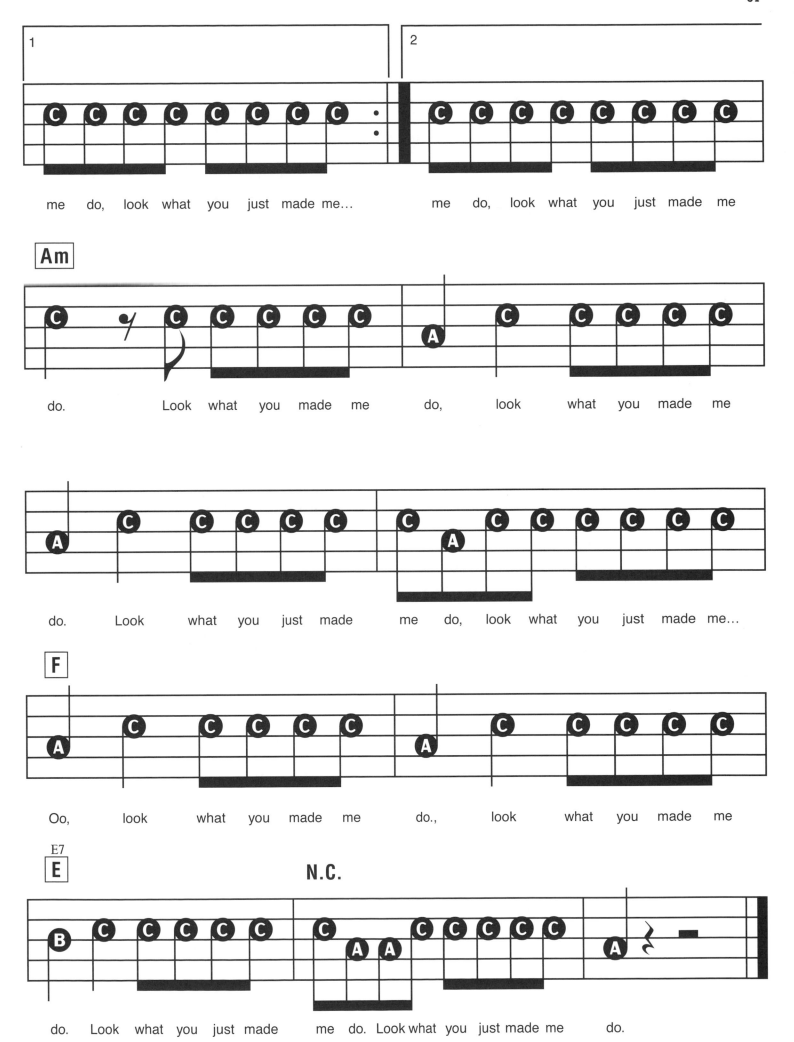

Let It Go

Registration 4
Rhythm: Ballad

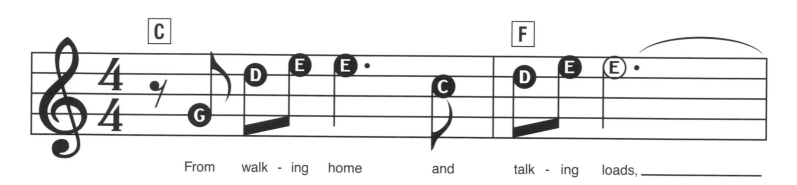

From walk - ing home and talk - ing loads, _____

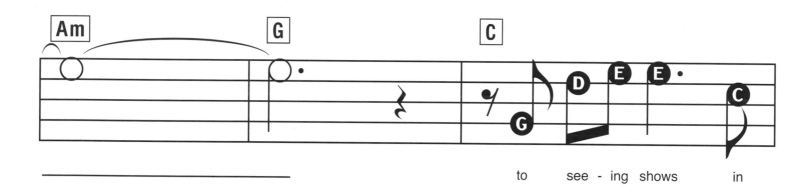

_____ to see - ing shows in

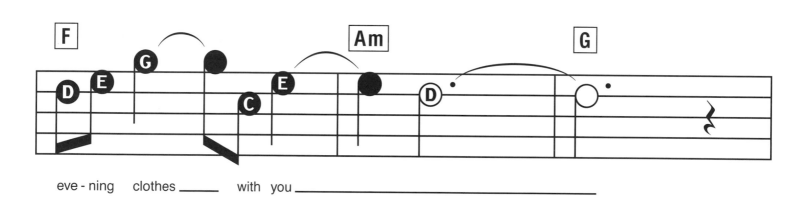

eve - ning clothes _____ with you _____

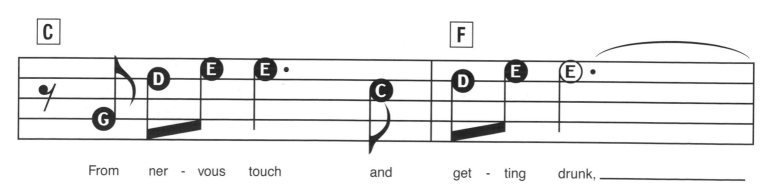

From ner - vous touch and get - ting drunk, _____

Words and Music by James Bay
and Paul Barry

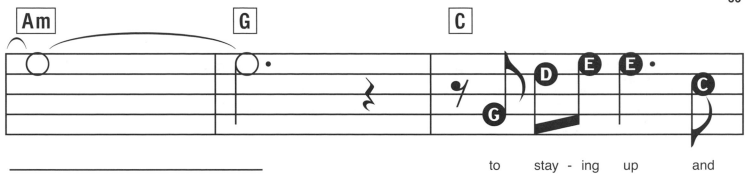

to stay - ing up and

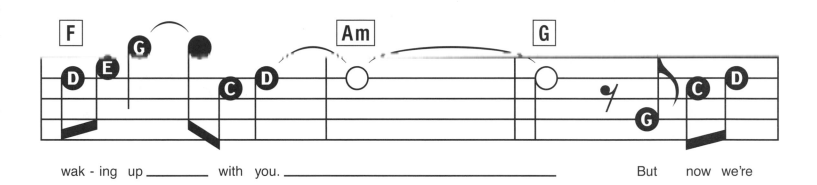

wak - ing up _____ with you. _____ But now we're

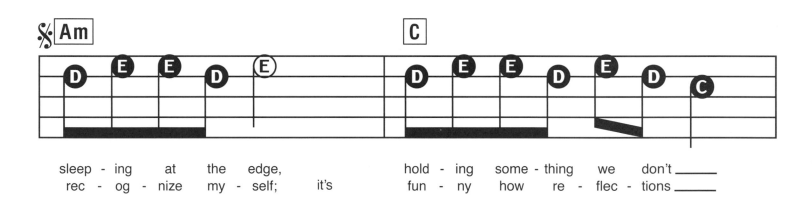

sleep - ing at the edge, hold - ing some - thing we don't _____
rec - og - nize my - self; it's fun - ny how re - flec - tions _____

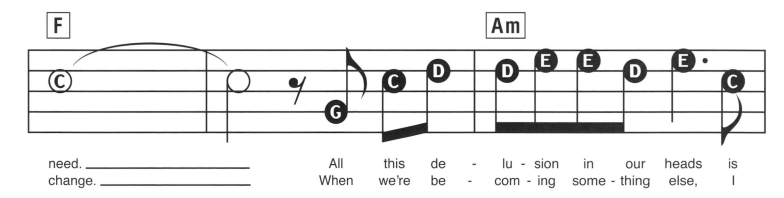

need. _____ All this de - lu - sion in our heads is
change. _____ When we're be - com - ing some - thing else, I

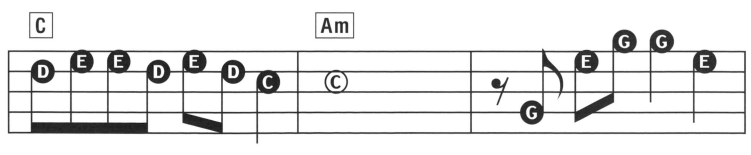

gon - na bring us to our _____ knees. }
think it's time to walk a - way. }

So, come on, let it

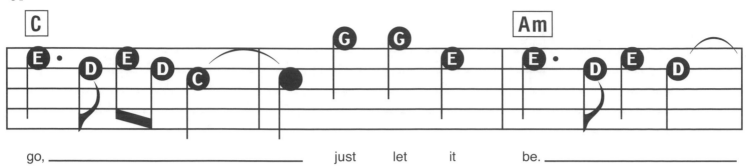

go, _____ just let it be. _____

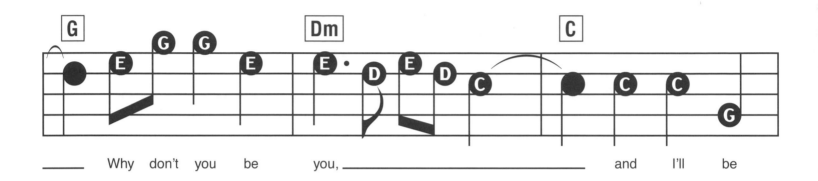

_____ Why don't you be you, _____ and I'll be

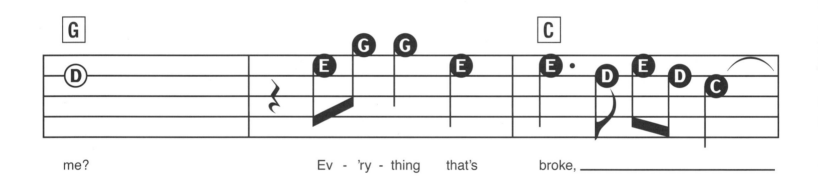

me? Ev - 'ry - thing that's broke, _____

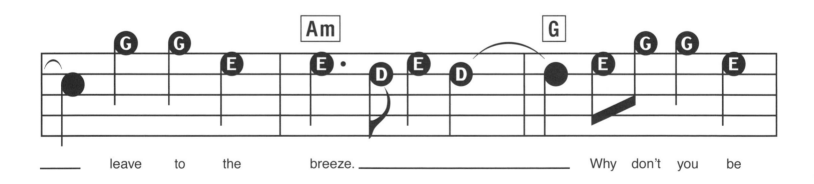

_____ leave to the breeze. _____ Why don't you be

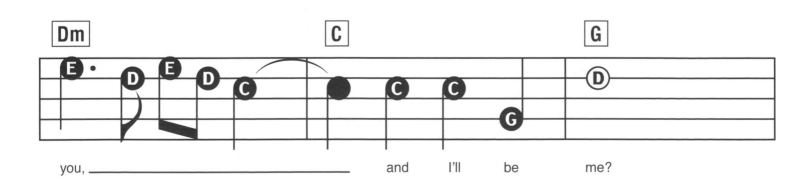

you, _____ and I'll be me?

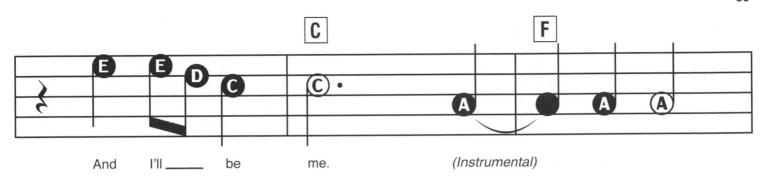

And I'll ___ be me. *(Instrumental)*

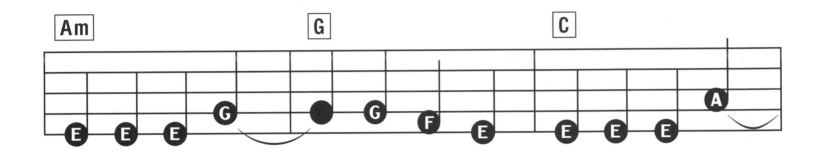

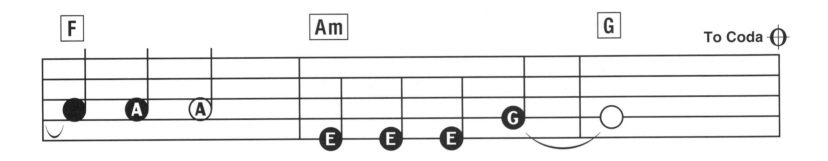

To Coda ⊕

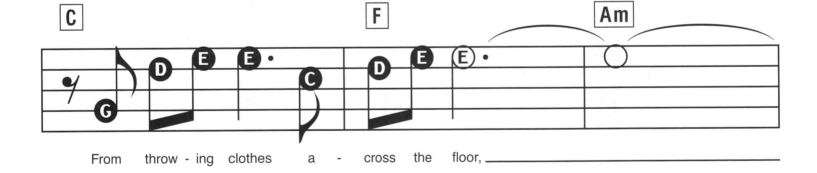

From throw - ing clothes a - cross the floor, _____

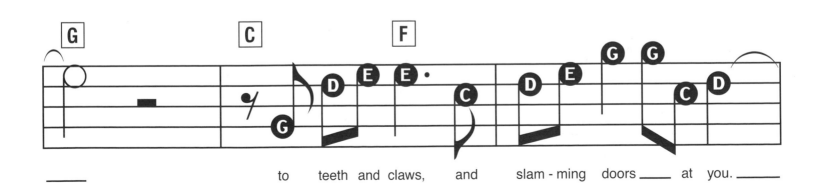

_____ to teeth and claws, and slam - ming doors ___ at you. ___

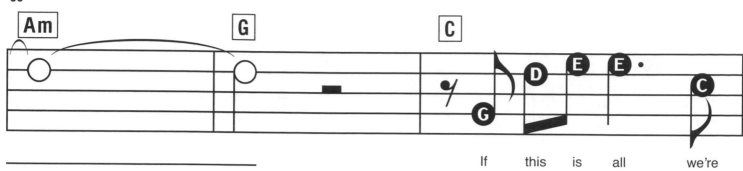

If this is all we're

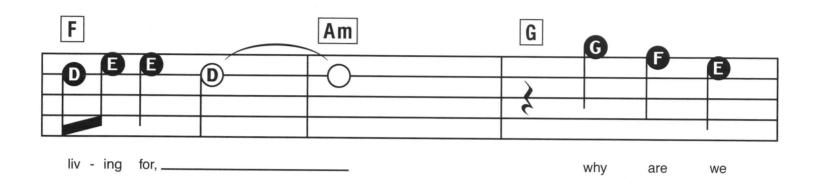

liv - ing for, _____ why are we

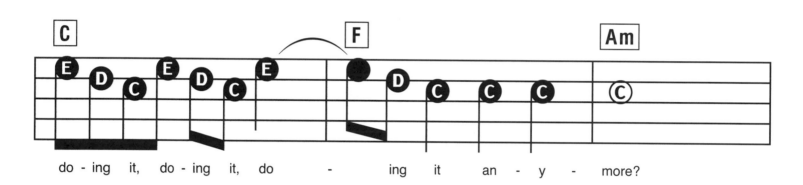

do - ing it, do - ing it, do - ing it an - y - more?

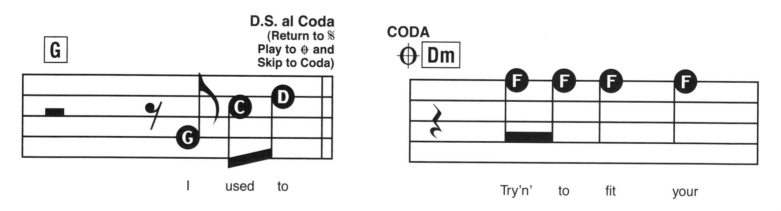

D.S. al Coda
(Return to 𝄋
Play to ⨁ and
Skip to Coda)

CODA

I used to

Try'n' to fit your

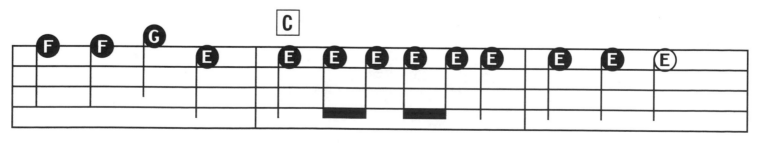

hand in - side of mine when we know it just don't be - long.

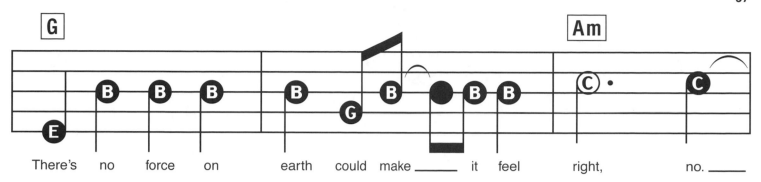

There's no force on earth could make _____ it feel right, no. _____

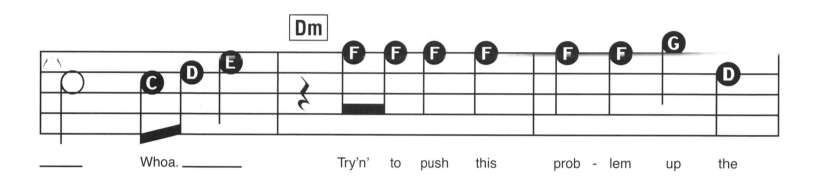

_____ Whoa. _____ Try'n' to push this prob-lem up the

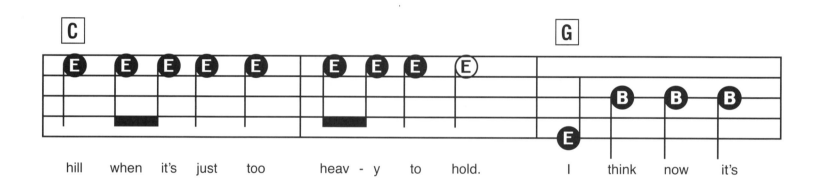

hill when it's just too heav-y to hold. I think now it's

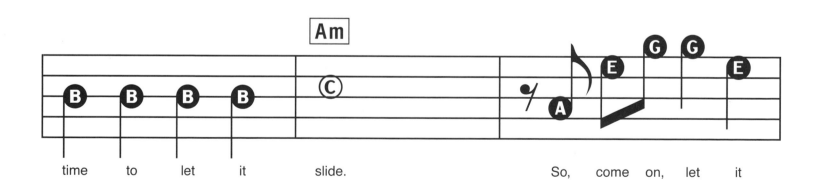

time to let it slide. So, come on, let it

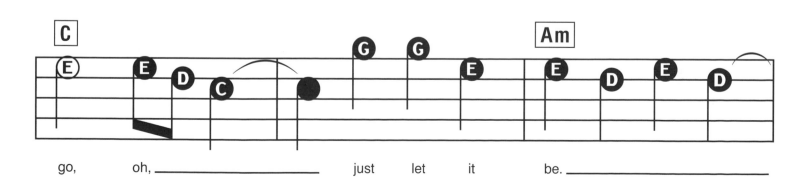

go, oh, _____ just let it be. _____

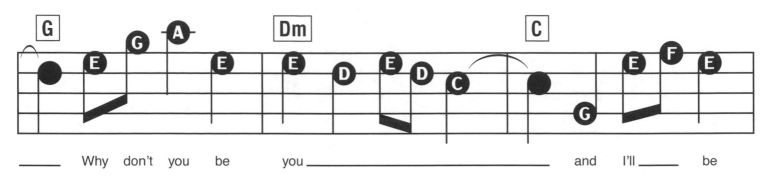

Why don't you be you _____ and I'll ____ be

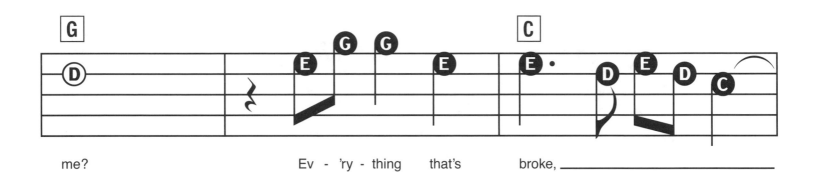

me? Ev - 'ry - thing that's broke, _____

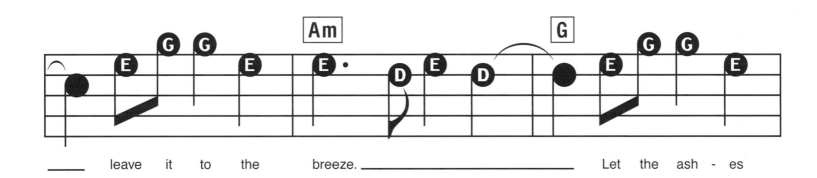

_____ leave it to the breeze. _____ Let the ash - es

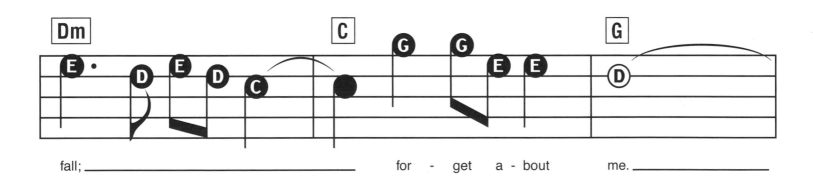

fall; _____ for - get a - bout me. _____

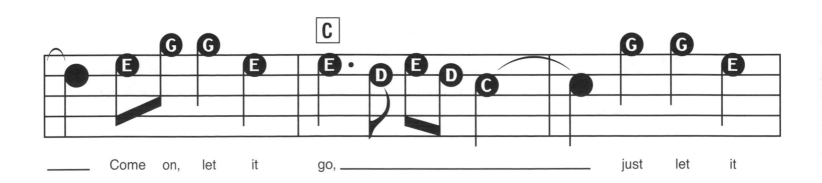

_____ Come on, let it go, _____ just let it

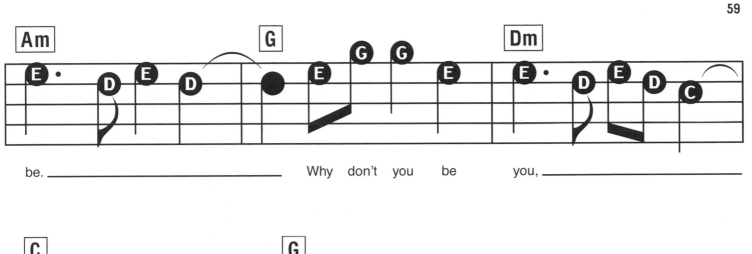

be. _____ Why don't you be you,

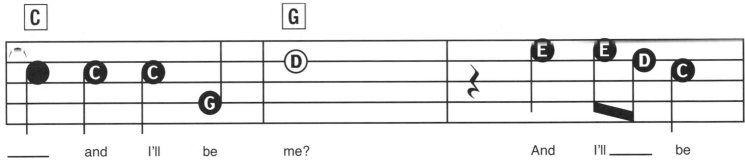

_____ and I'll be me? And I'll ____ be

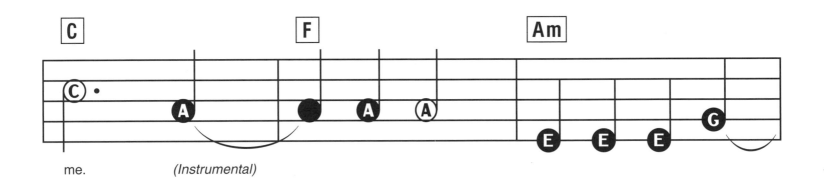

me. (Instrumental)

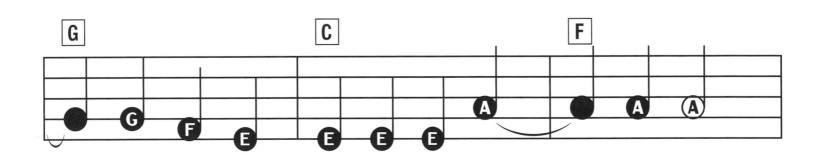

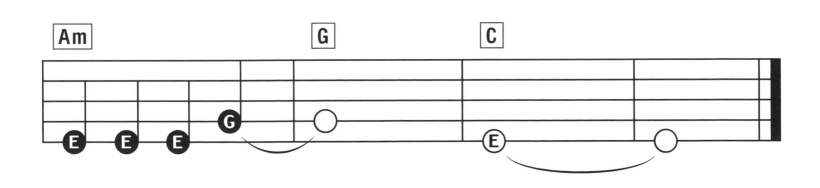

Mercy

Registration 8
Rhythm: Ballad or Rock

Words and Music by Shawn Mendes,
Teddy Geiger, Danny Parker and Ilsey Juber

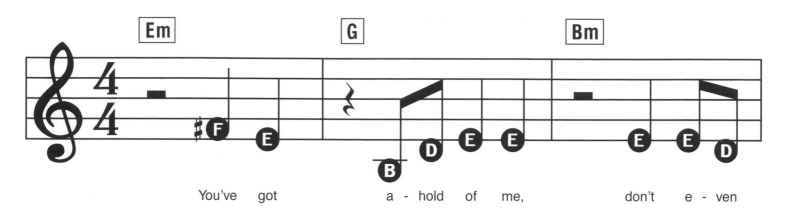

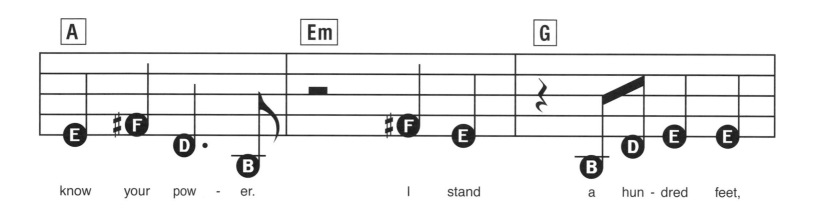

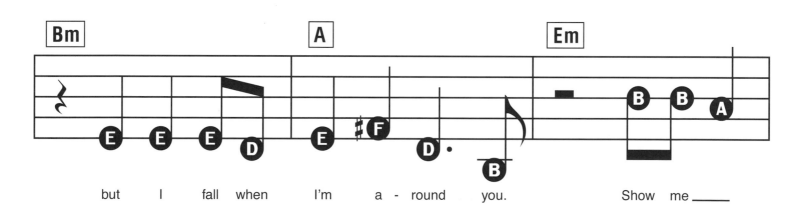

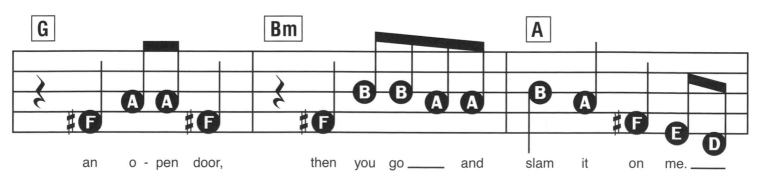

61

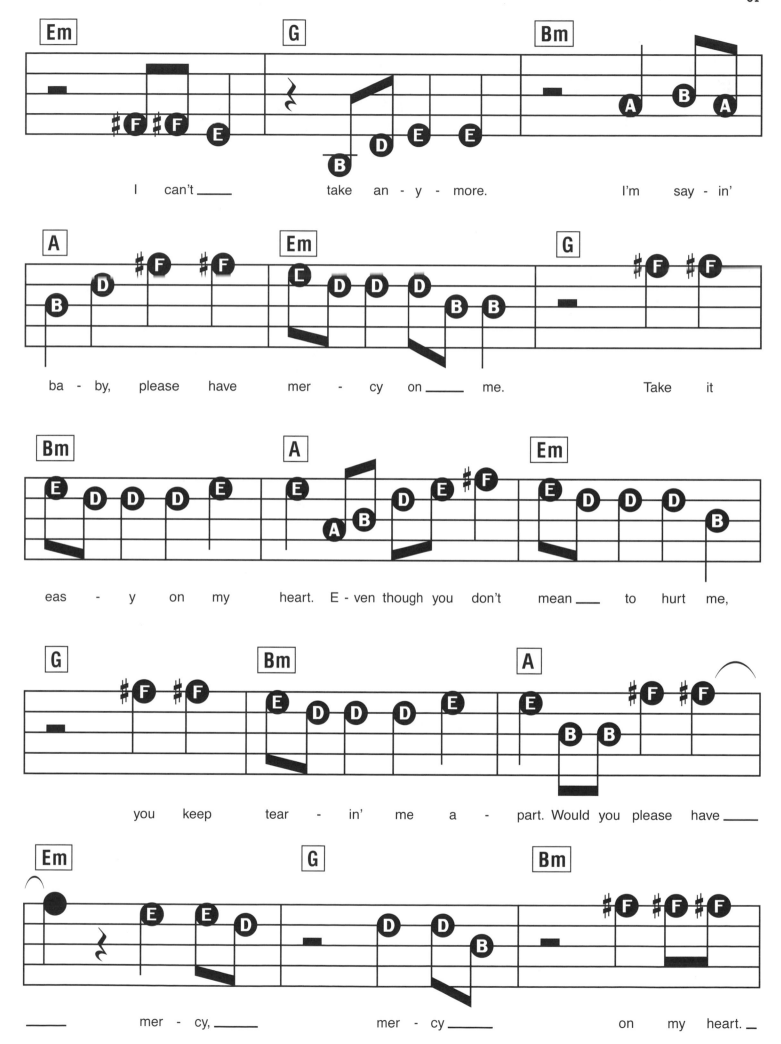

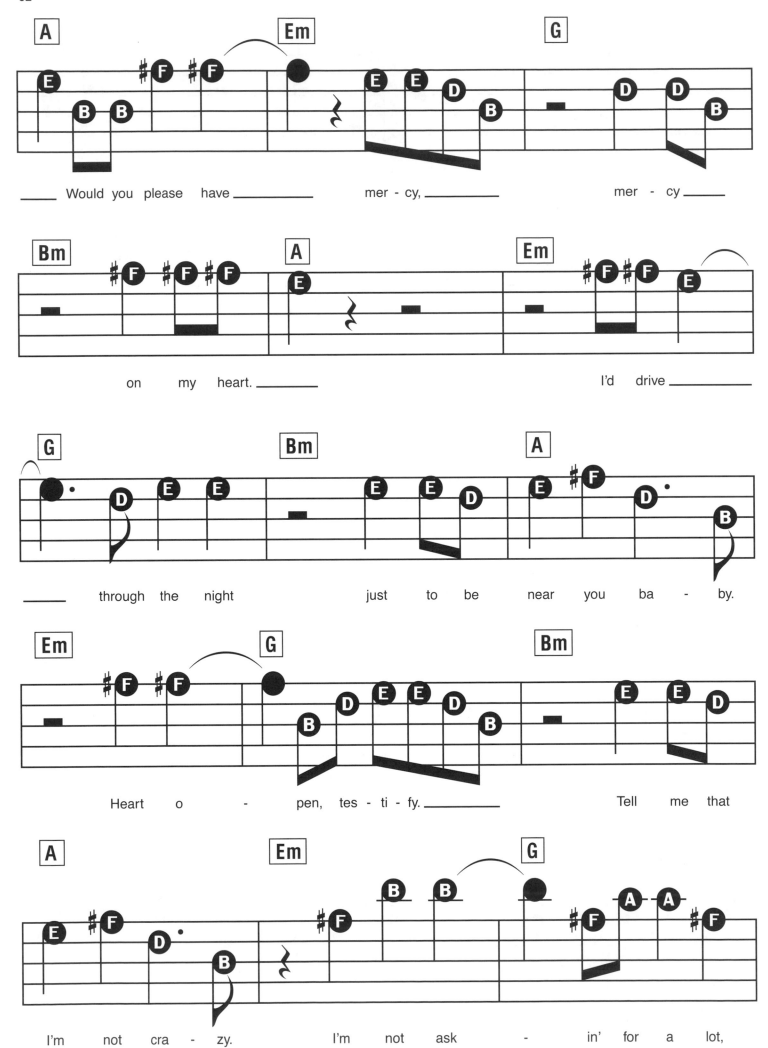

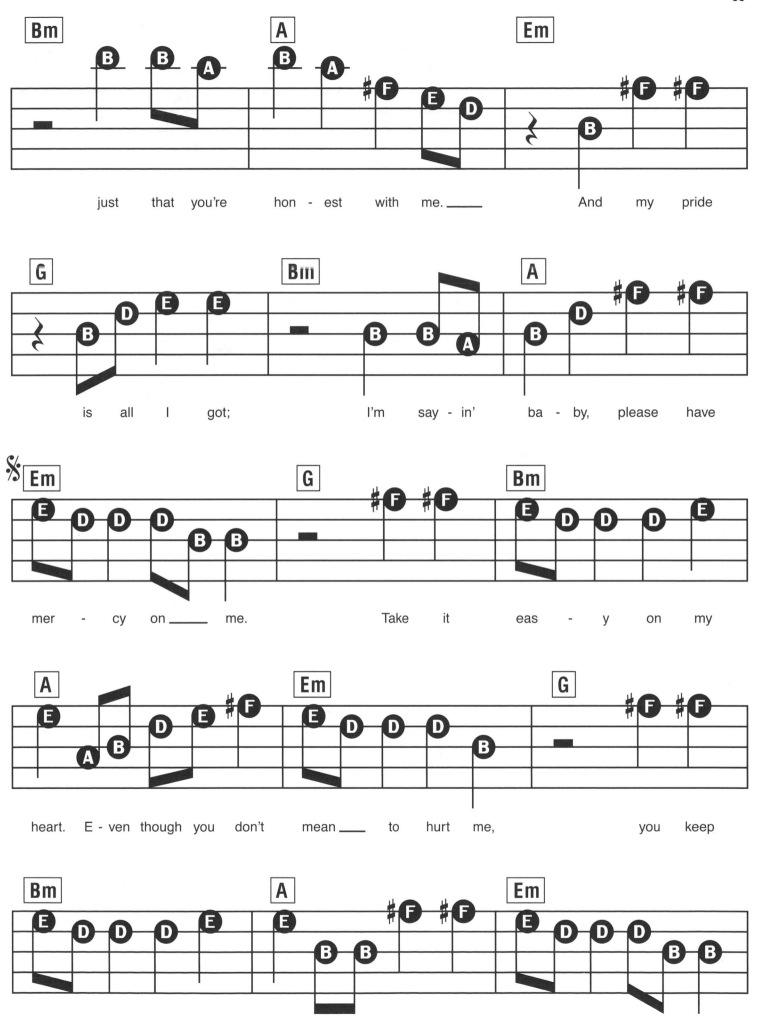

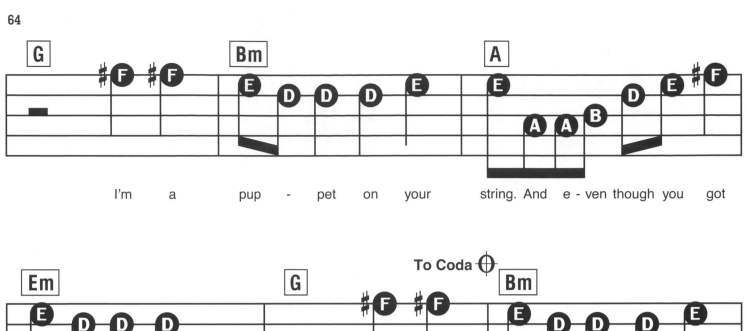

I'm a pup - pet on your string. And e - ven though you got

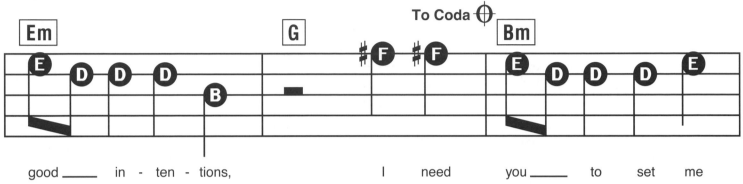

good _____ in - ten - tions, I need you _____ to set me

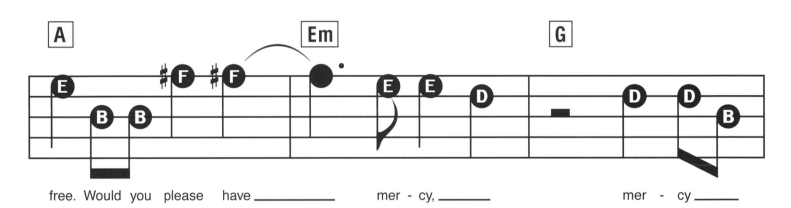

free. Would you please have _____ mer - cy, _____ mer - cy _____

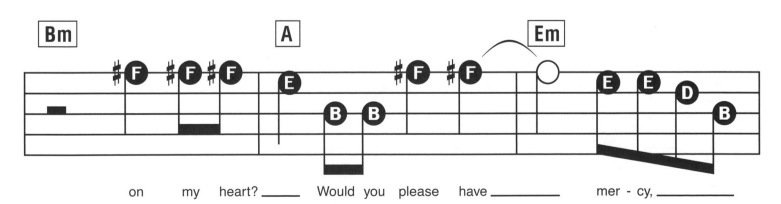

on my heart? _____ Would you please have _____ mer - cy, _____

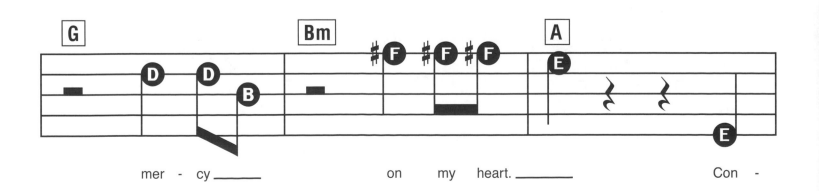

mer - cy _____ on my heart. _____ Con -

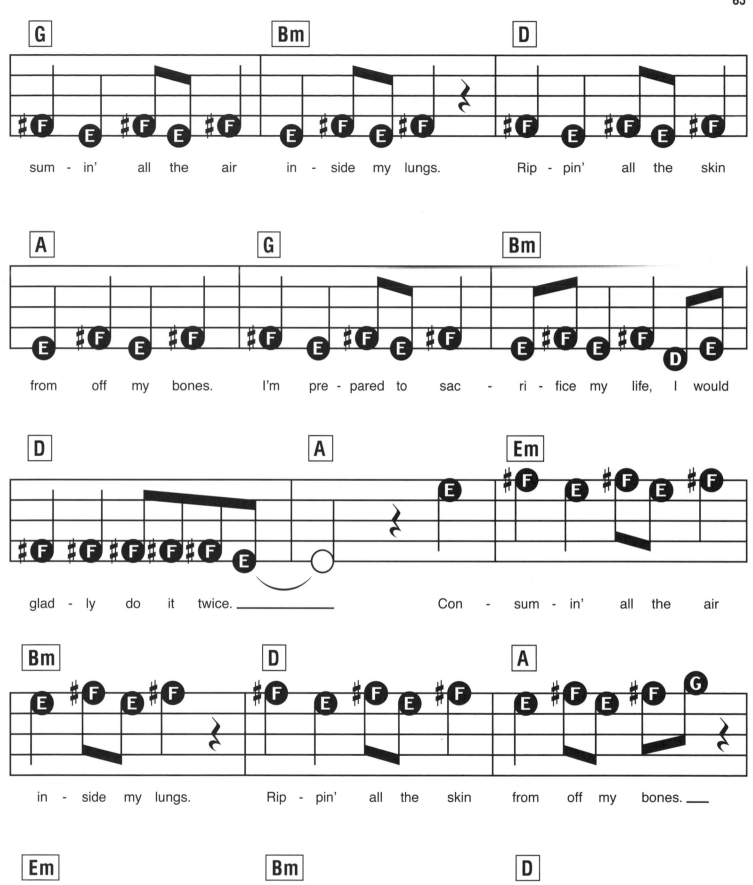

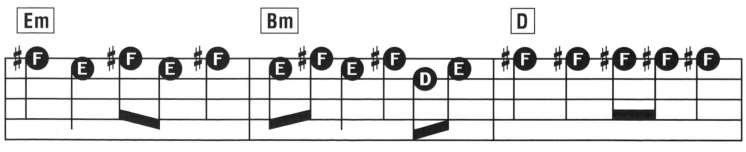

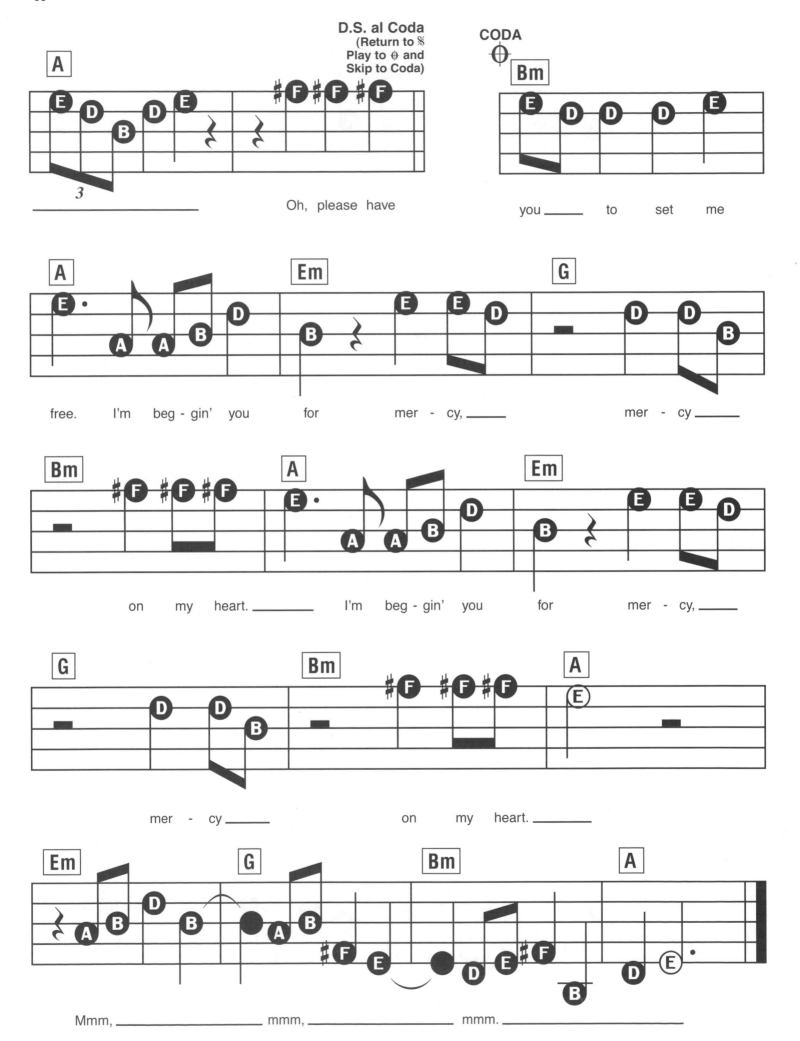

Million Reasons

Registration 4
Rhythm: Rock or 8-Beat

Words and Music by Stefani Germanotta,
Mark Ronson and Hillary Lindsey

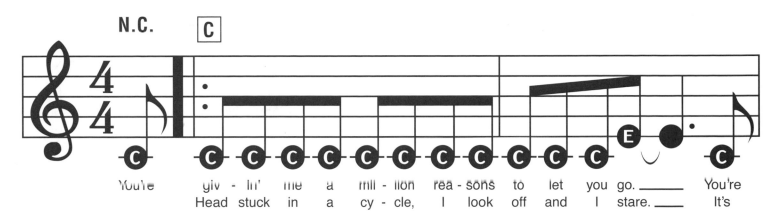

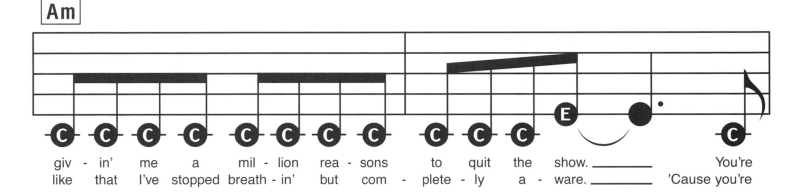

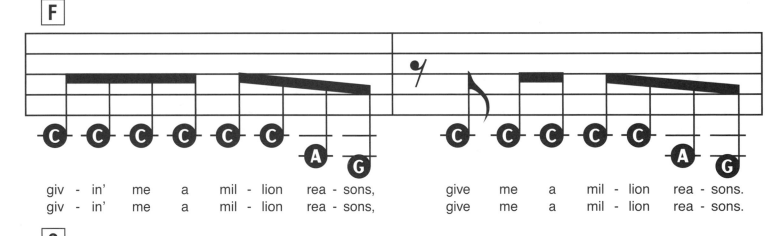

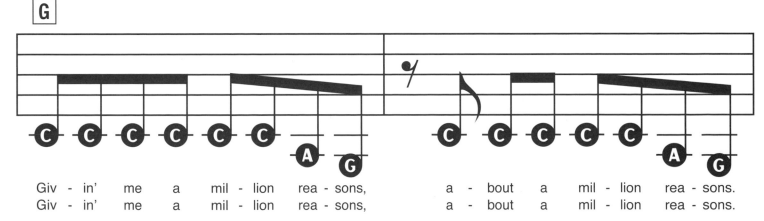

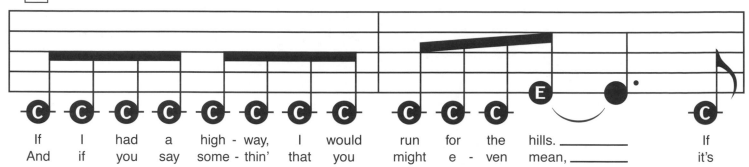

C

If   I   had   a   high - way,   I   would   run   for   the   hills. _____   If

And   if   you   say   some - thin'   that   you   might   e - ven   mean, _____   it's

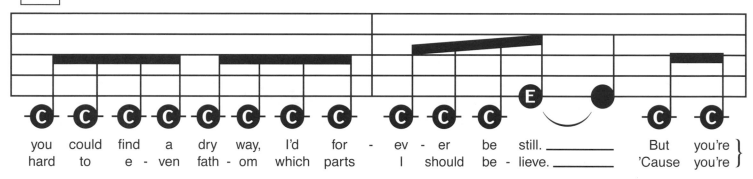

Am

you   could   find   a   dry   way,   I'd   for - ev - er   be   still. _____   But   you're

hard   to   e - ven   fath - om   which   parts   I   should   be - lieve. _____   'Cause   you're }

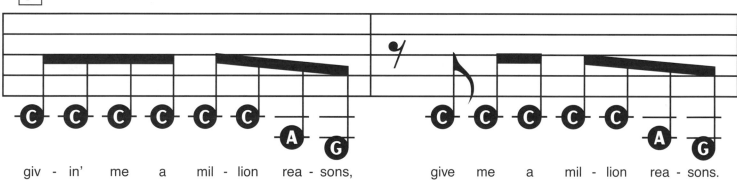

F

giv - in'   me   a   mil - lion   rea - sons,   give   me   a   mil - lion   rea - sons.

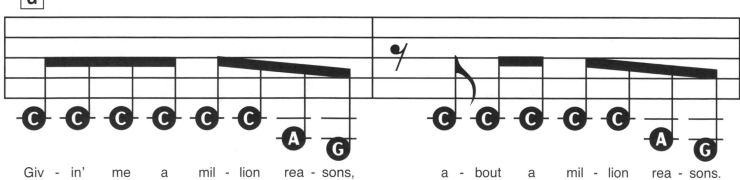

G

Giv - in'   me   a   mil - lion   rea - sons,   a - bout   a   mil - lion   rea - sons.

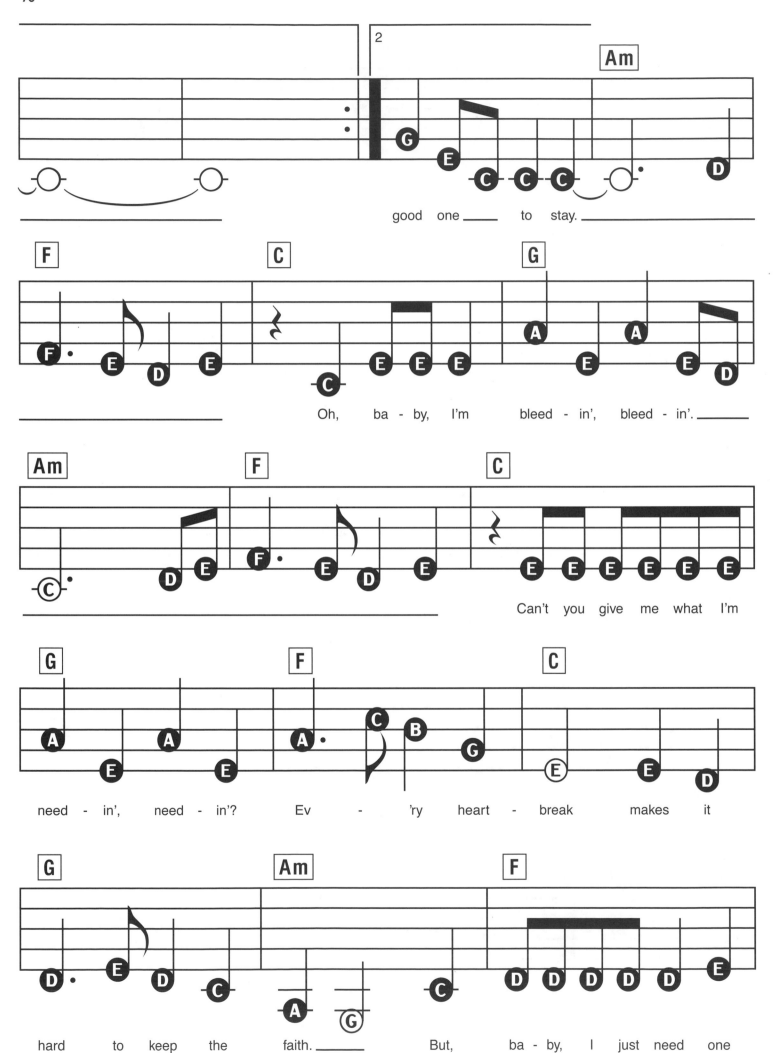

D.S. al Coda
(Return to %
Play to ⊕ and
Skip to Coda)

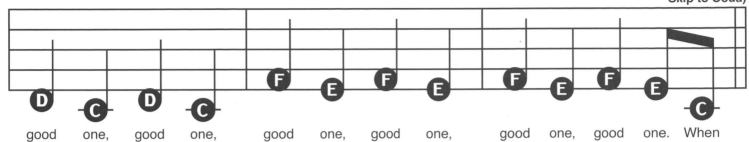

good one, good one, good one, good one, good one, good one. When

CODA

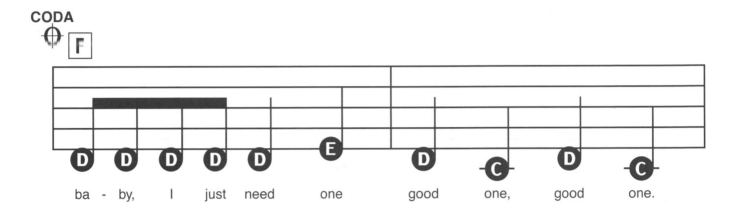

ba - by, I just need one good one, good one.

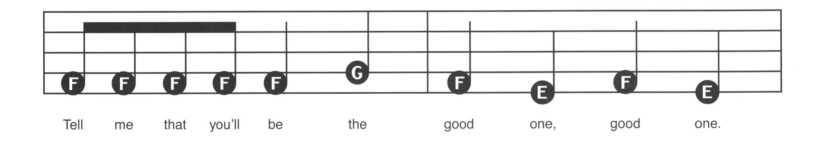

Tell me that you'll be the good one, good one.

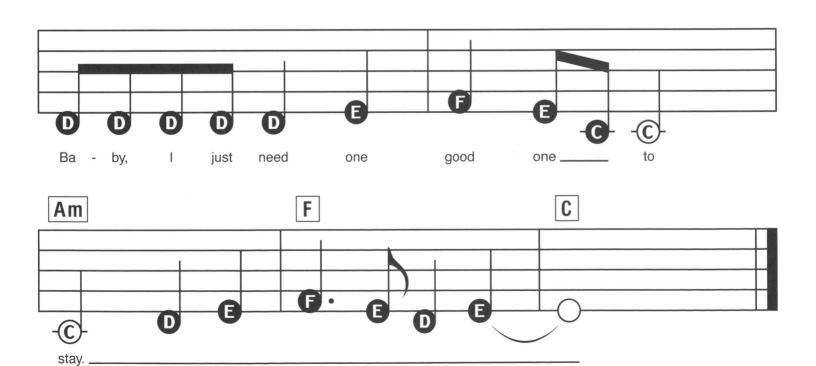

Ba - by, I just need one good one _____ to

| Am | F | C |

stay. _____

One Call Away

Registration 8
Rhythm: Rock or 8-Beat

Words and Music by Charlie Puth,
Breyan Isaac, Matt Prime, Justin Franks,
Blake Anthony Carter and Maureen McDonald

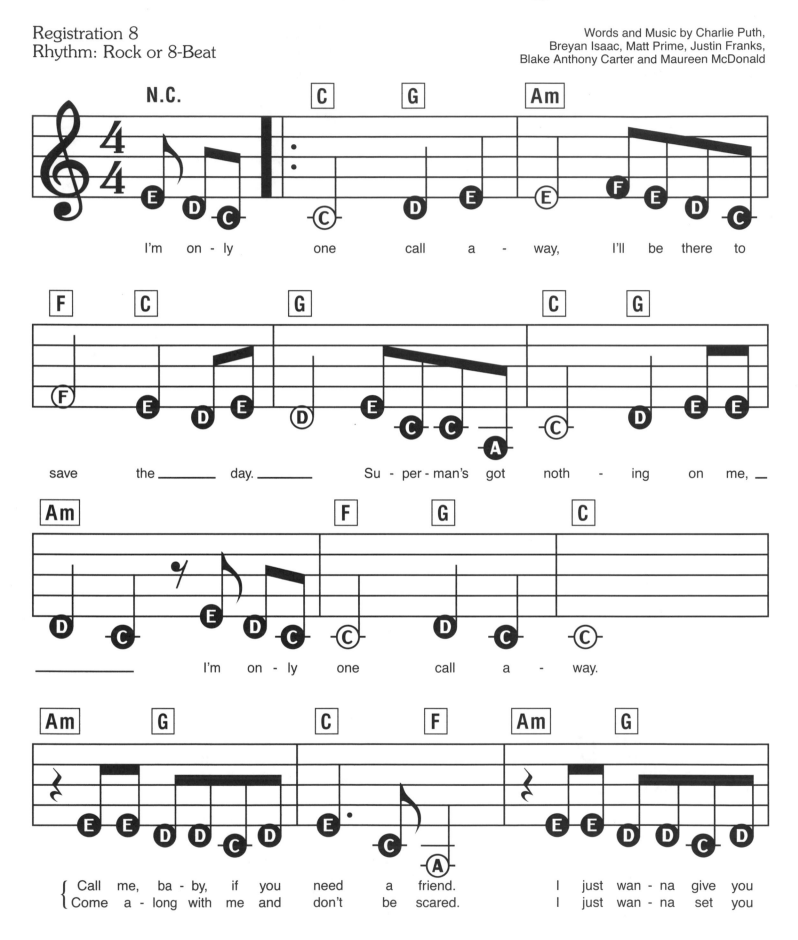

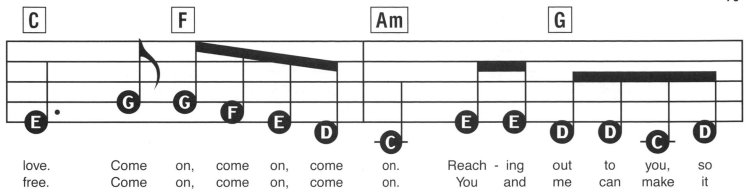

love.   Come   on,   come   on,   come   on.   Reach - ing   out   to   you,   so
free.   Come   on,   come   on,   come   on.   You   and   me   can   make   so   it

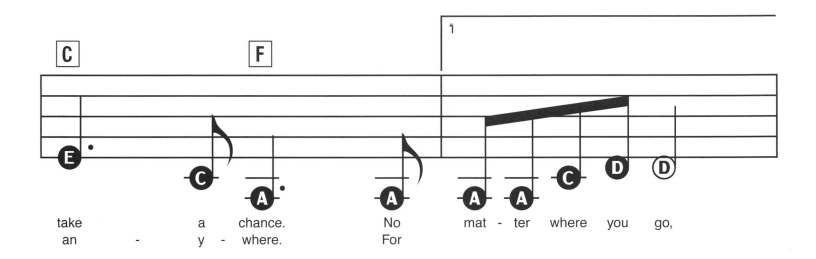

take   a   chance.   No   mat - ter   where   you   go,
an   -   y   -   where.   For

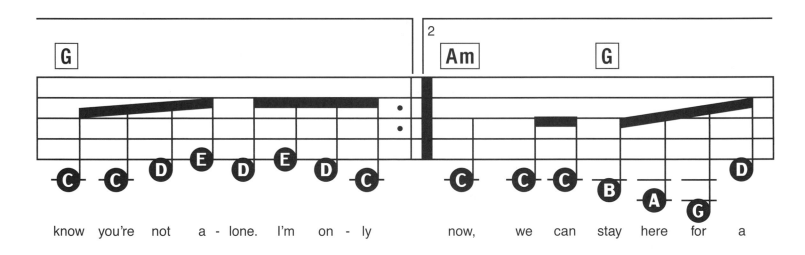

know   you're   not   a - lone.   I'm   on - ly   now,   we   can   stay   here   for   a

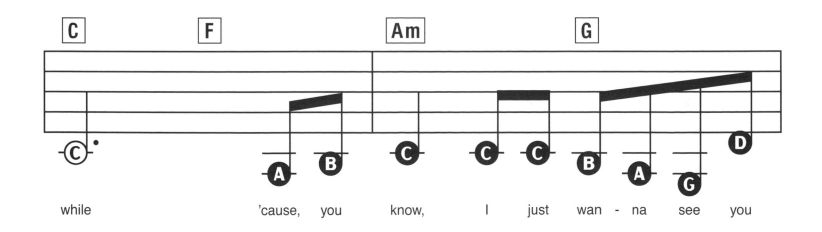

while   'cause,   you   know,   I   just   wan - na   see   you

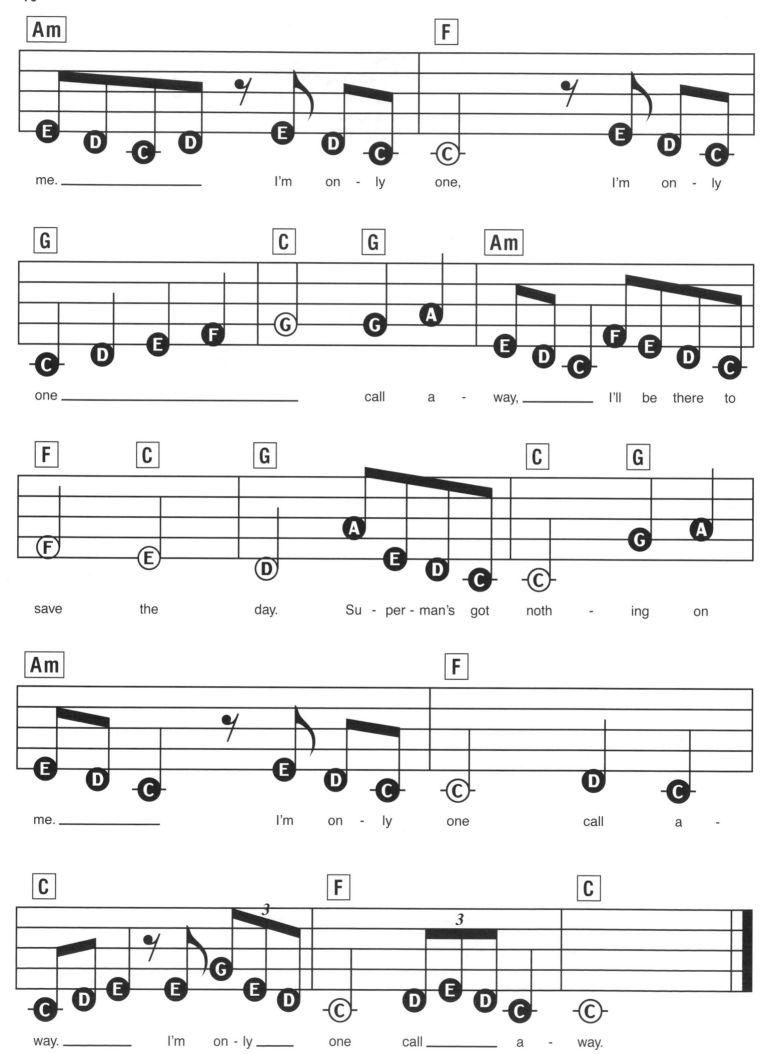

Shape of You

Registration 5
Rhythm: Pop or Techno

Words and Music by Ed Sheeran,
Kevin Briggs, Kandi Burruss, Tameka Cottle,
Steve Mac and Johnny McDaid

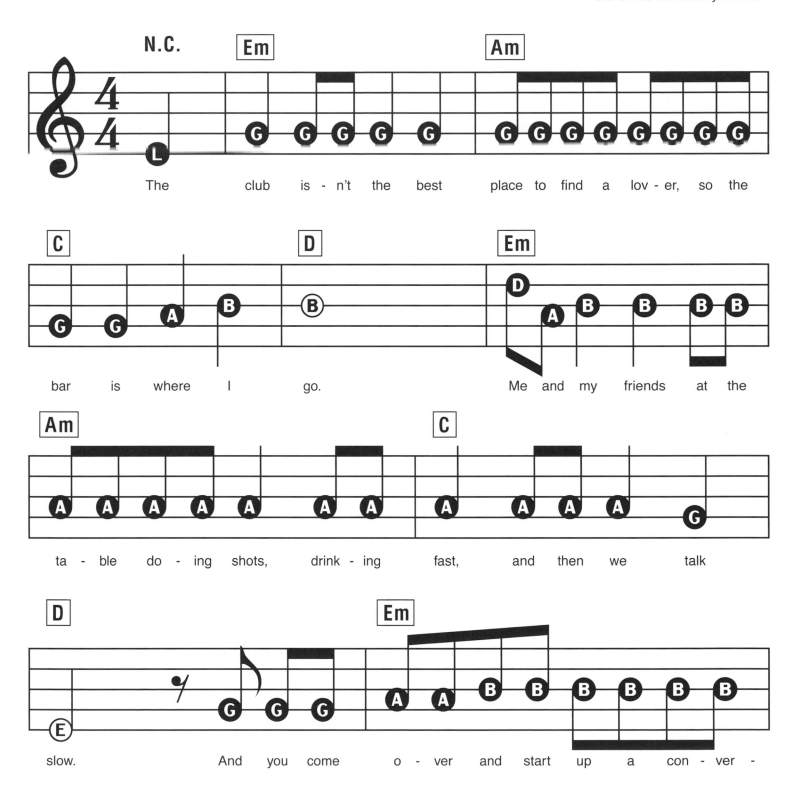

Am ... **C**

B   B   B   B   B   B   D   A   B   A   A   A

sa - tion   with   just   me,   and   trust   me,   I'll   give   it   a

D ... **Em**

B   A   G   G   G   G   D   A   B   B

chance.   Now ____ take   my   hand,   stop,   put   Van   the

Am ... **C**

A   A   A   A   A   A   A   A   A   G   E

Man   on   the   juke - box   and   then   we   start   to   dance,

D ... **Em** ... **Am**

B   B   B   D   E   E   E   E   E   D   E   B   A

and   now   I'm   sing - ing   like,   Girl,   you   know   I   want   your   love.

C ... **D** ... **Em**

G   A   B   A   G   E   G   B   A   G   A   E   D   A   B

Your   love   was   hand - made   for   some - bod - y   like ____ me.   Come   on,   now,

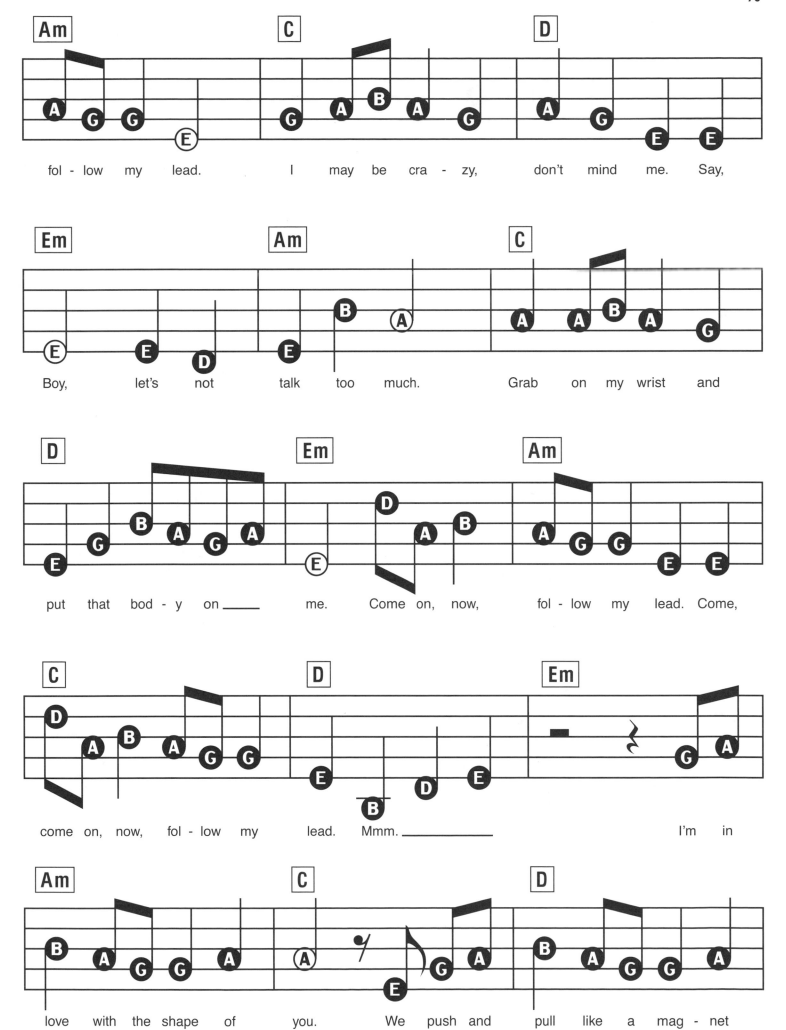

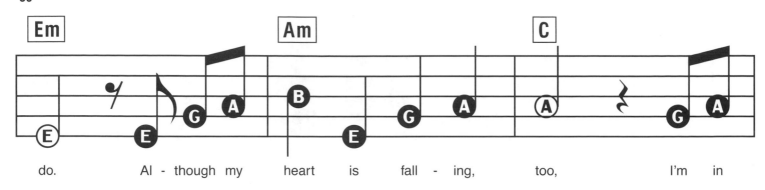

do. Al - though my heart is fall - ing, too, I'm in

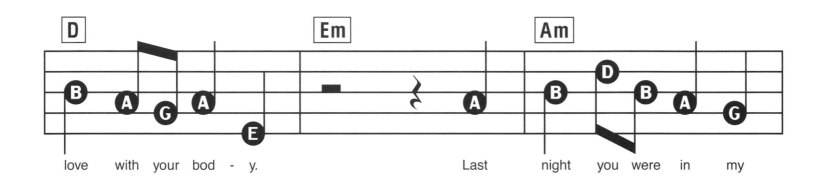

love with your bod - y. Last night you were in my

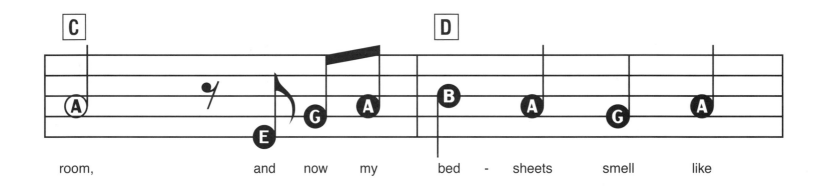

room, and now my bed - sheets smell like

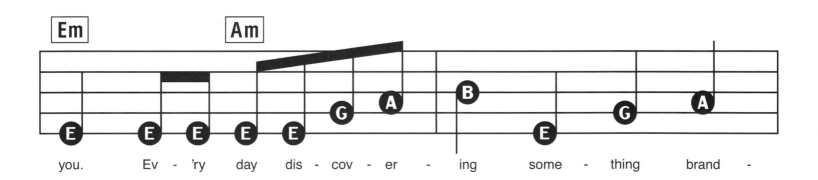

you. Ev - 'ry day dis - cov - er - ing some - thing brand -

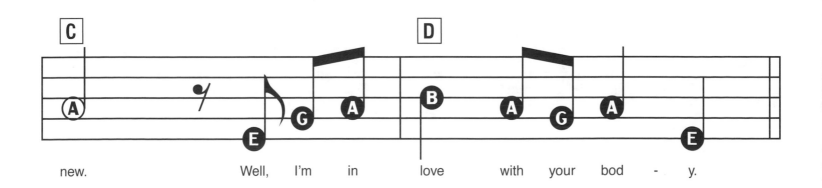

new. Well, I'm in love with your bod - y.

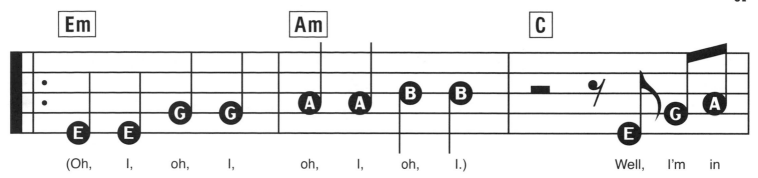

(Oh, I, oh, I, oh, I, oh, I.) Well, I'm in

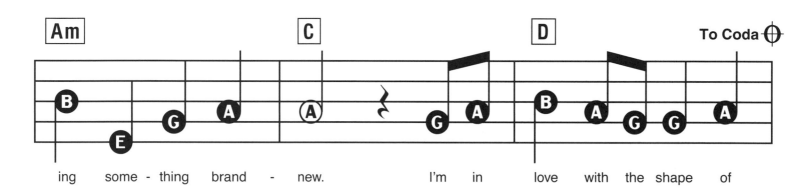

love with your bod - y. Ev - 'ry day dis - cov - er -

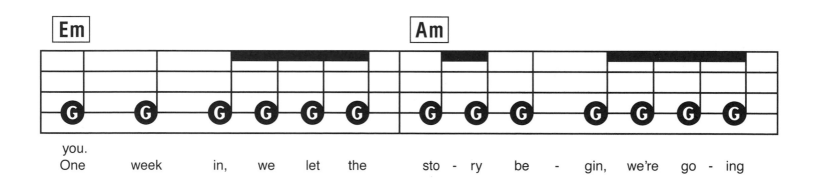

ing some - thing brand - new. I'm in love with the shape of

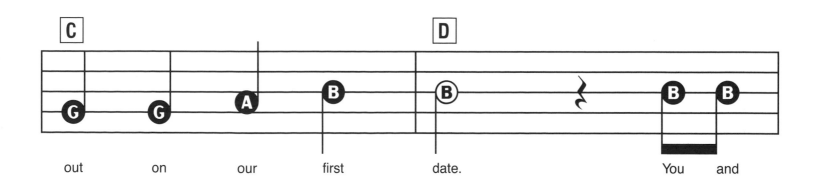

you.
One week in, we let the sto - ry be - gin, we're go - ing

out on our first date. You and

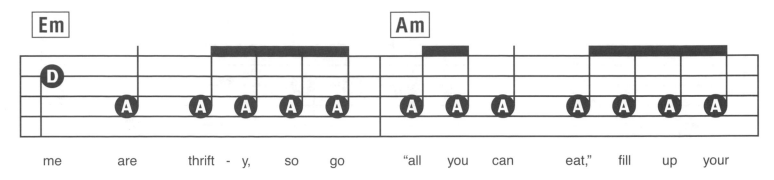

me   are   thrift - y,   so   go   "all   you   can   eat,"   fill   up   your

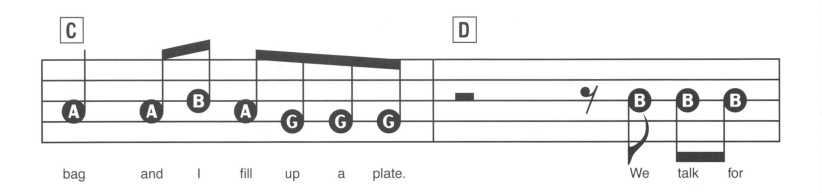

bag   and   I   fill   up   a   plate.   We   talk   for

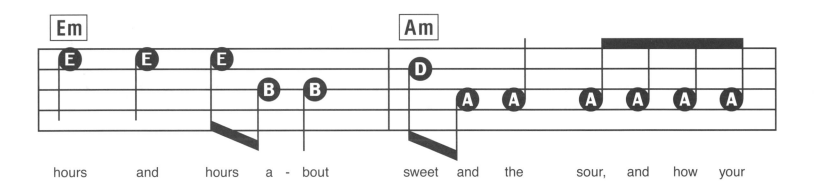

hours   and   hours   a - bout   sweet   and   the   sour,   and   how   your

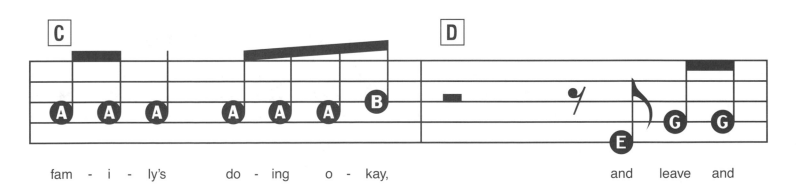

fam - i - ly's   do - ing   o - kay,   and   leave   and

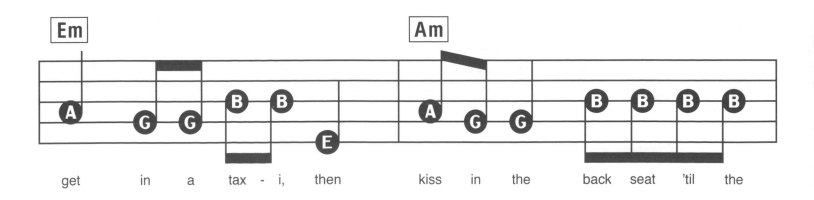

get   in   a   tax - i,   then   kiss   in   the   back   seat   'til   the

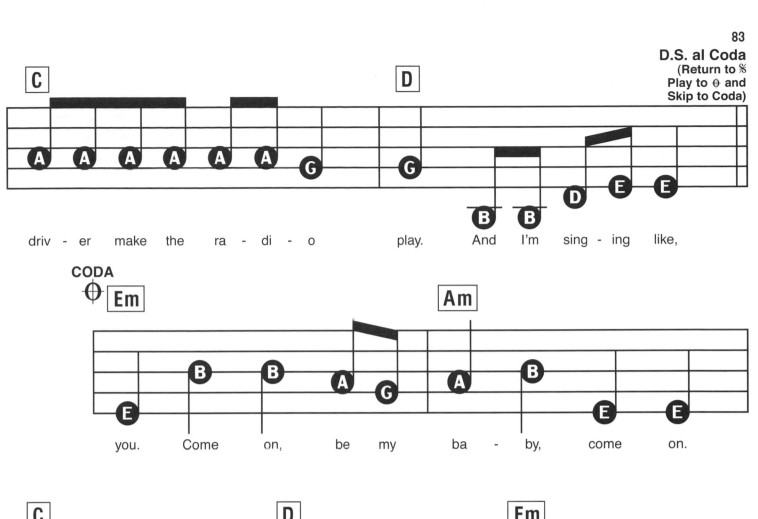

driv - er make the ra - di - o play. And I'm sing - ing like,

CODA

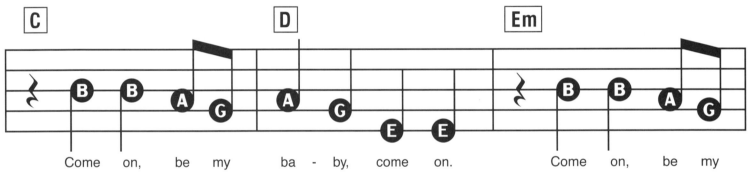

you. Come on, be my ba - by, come on.

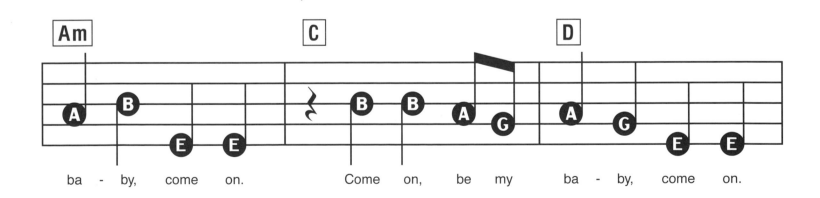

Come on, be my ba - by, come on. Come on, be my

ba - by, come on. Come on, be my ba - by, come on.

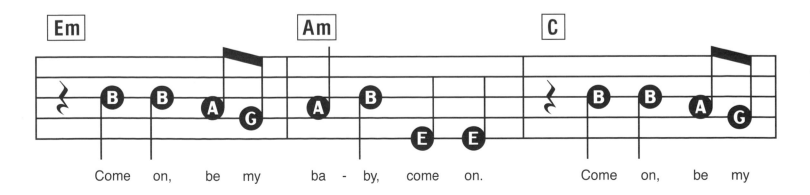

Come on, be my ba - by, come on. Come on, be my

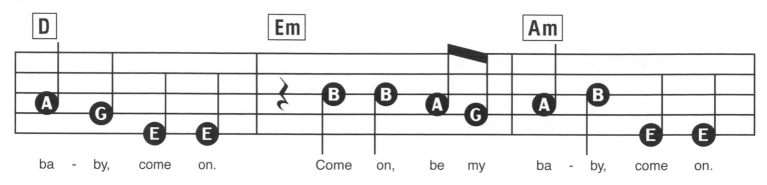

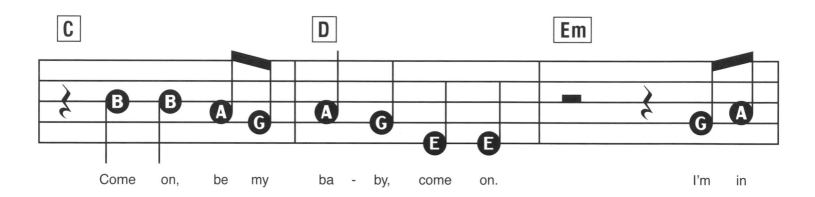

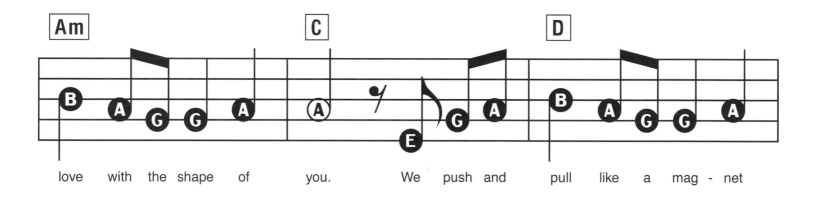

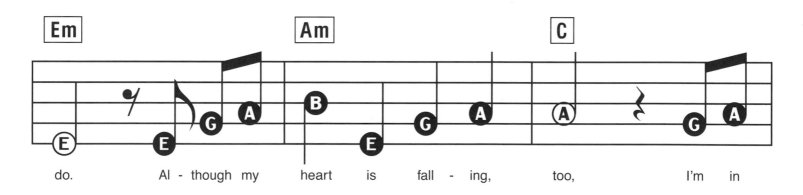

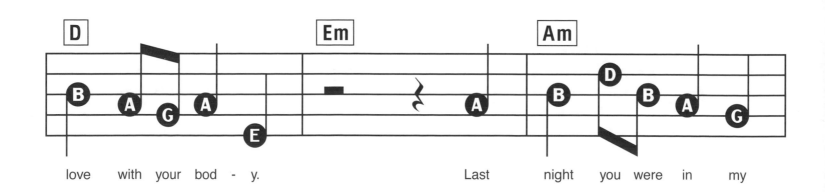

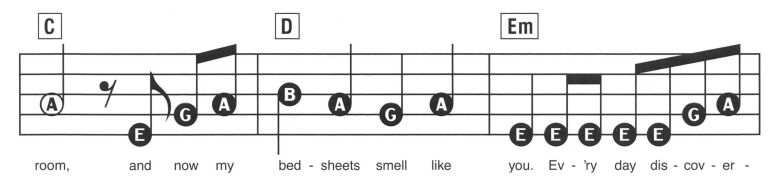

room, and now my bed - sheets smell like you. Ev - 'ry day dis - cov - er -

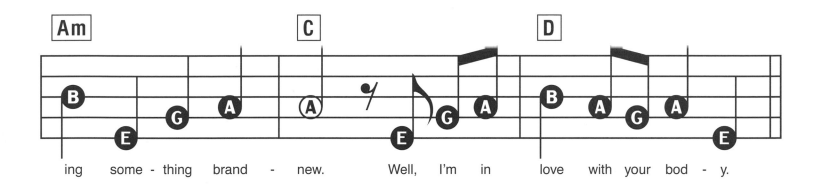

ing some - thing brand - new. Well, I'm in love with your bod - y.

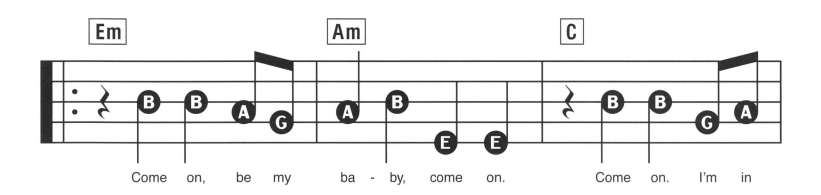

Come on, be my ba - by, come on. Come on. I'm in

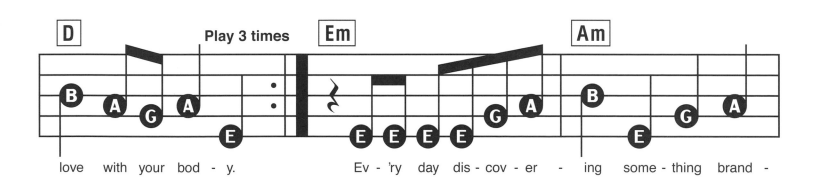

Play 3 times

love with your bod - y. Ev - 'ry day dis - cov - er - ing some - thing brand -

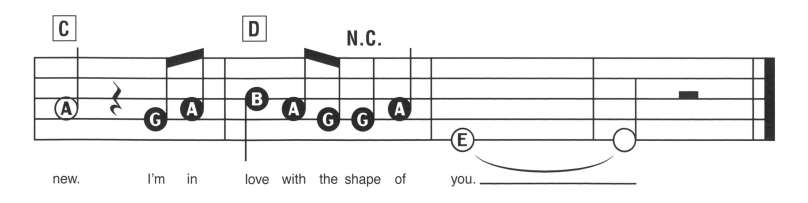

N.C.

new. I'm in love with the shape of you. _____

Say You Won't Let Go

Registration 8
Rhythm: Ballad

Words and Music by Steven Solomon,
James Arthur and Neil Ormandy

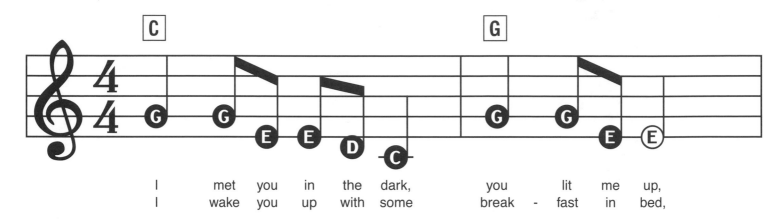

I met you in the dark, you lit me up,
I wake you up with some break - fast in bed,

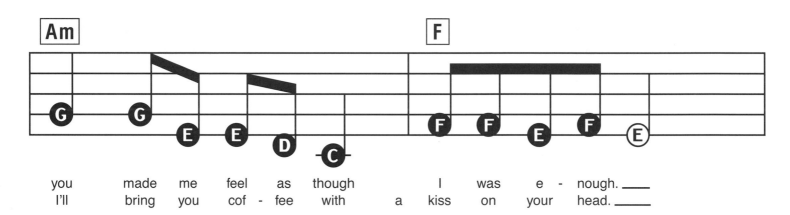

you made me feel as though I was e - nough. _____
I'll bring you cof - fee with a kiss on your head. _____

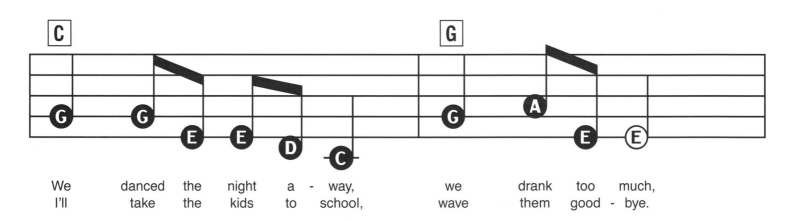

We danced the night a - way, we drank too much,
I'll take the kids to school, wave them good - bye.

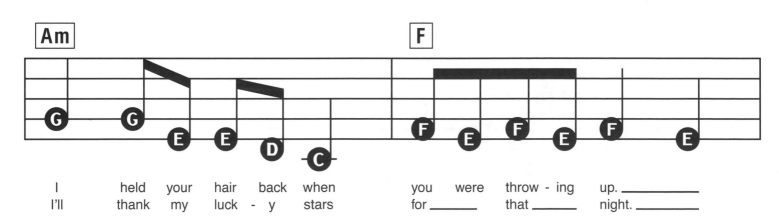

I held your hair back when you were throw - ing up. _____
I'll thank my luck - y stars for _____ that _____ night. _____

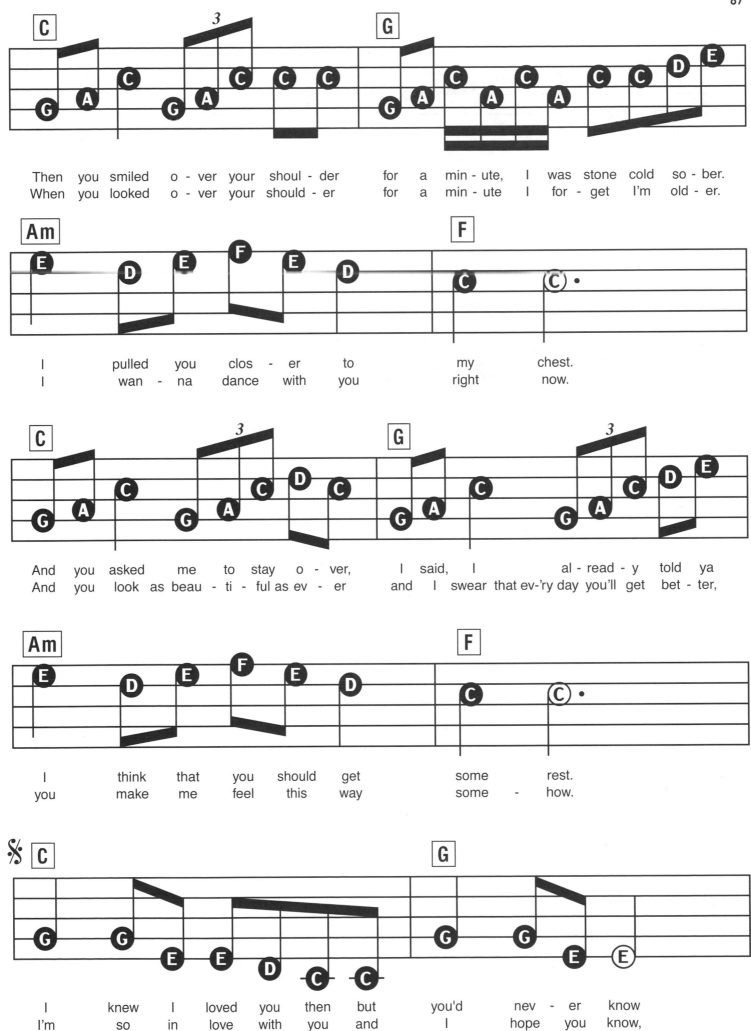

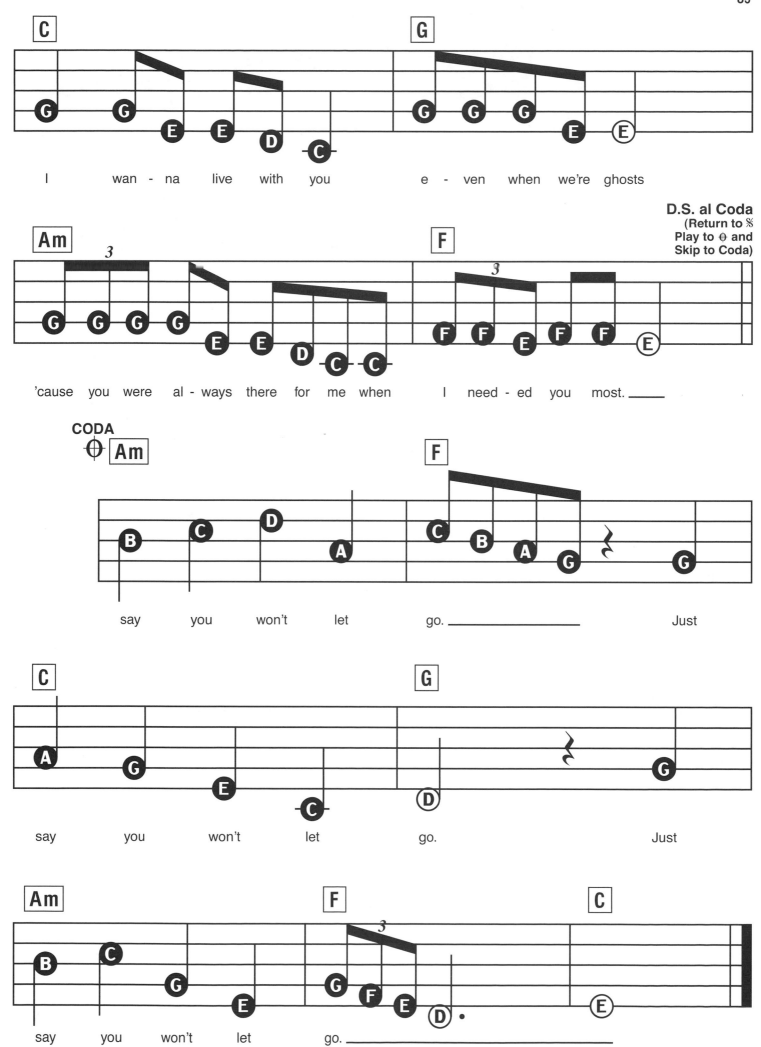

I wan-na live with you e-ven when we're ghosts

D.S. al Coda
(Return to %
Play to ⊕ and
Skip to Coda)

'cause you were al-ways there for me when I need-ed you most._____

CODA
⊕ Am
say you won't let go. _____ Just

say you won't let go. Just

say you won't let go. _____

Send My Love
(To Your New Lover)

Registration 4
Rhythm: Pop

Words and Music by Adele Adkins,
Max Martin and Shellback

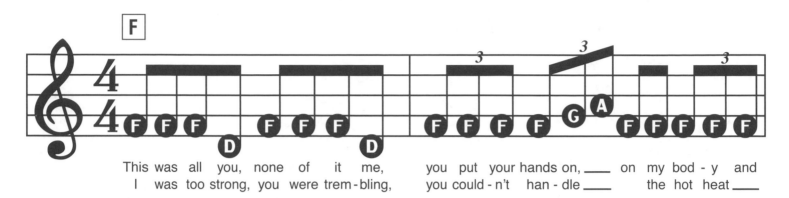

This was all you, none of it me, you put your hands on, ___ on my bod - y and
I was too strong, you were trem - bling, you could - n't han - dle ___ the hot heat ___

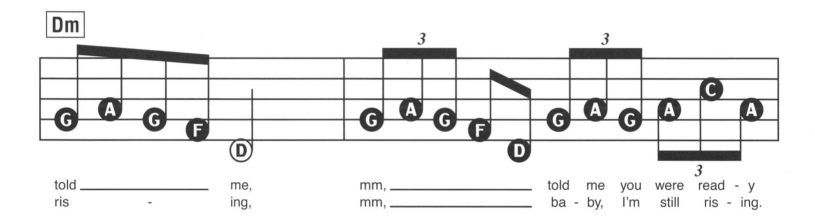

told _____ me, mm, _____ told me you were read - y
ris - ing, mm, _____ ba - by, I'm still ris - ing.

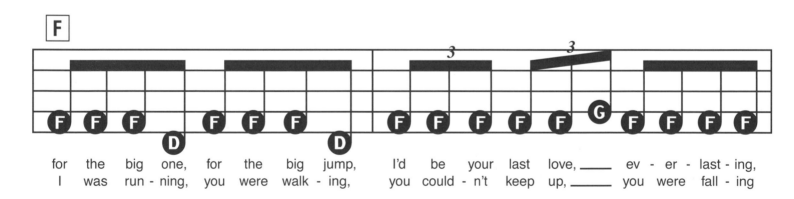

for the big one, for the big jump, I'd be your last love, ___ ev - er - last - ing,
I was run - ning, you were walk - ing, you could - n't keep up, ___ you were fall - ing

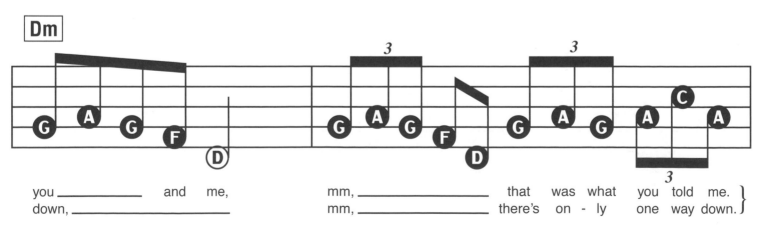

you _____ and me, mm, _____ that was what you told me.
down, _____ mm, _____ there's on - ly one way down.

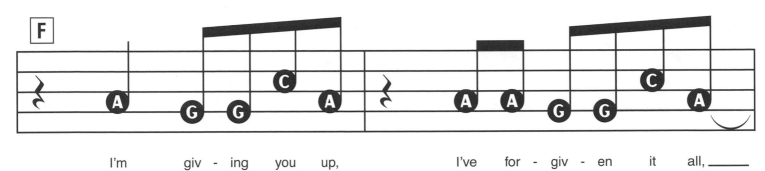

I'm giv - ing you up, I've for - giv - en it all, _____

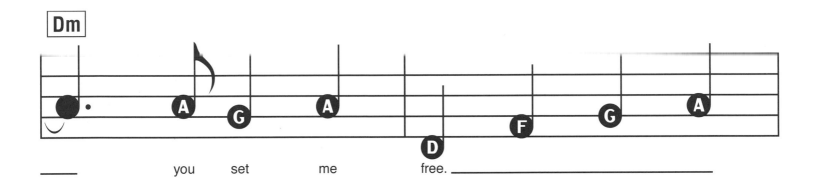

_____ you set me free. _____

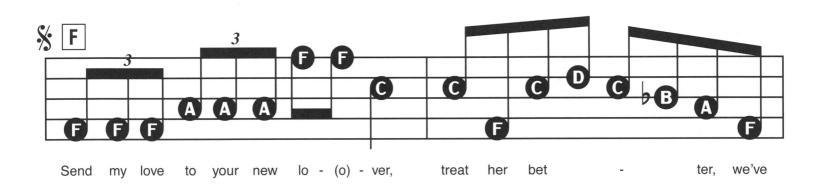

Send my love to your new lo - (o) - ver, treat her bet - ter, we've

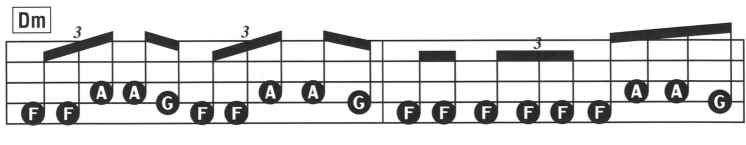

got - ta let go of all of our ghosts, __ we both know we ain't kids no more. __

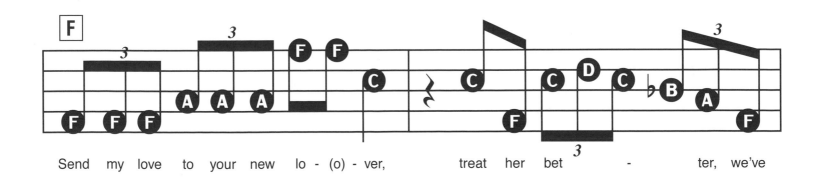

Send my love to your new lo - (o) - ver, treat her bet - ter, we've

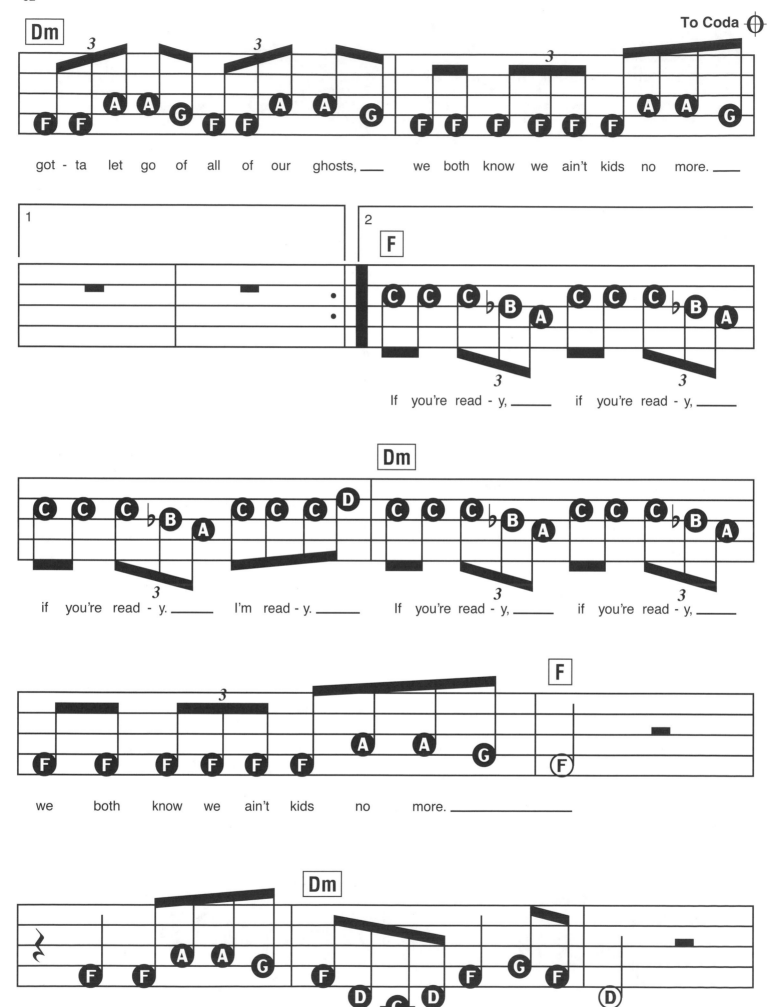

To Coda ⊕

got - ta let go of all of our ghosts, ___ we both know we ain't kids no more. ___

If you're read - y, ___ if you're read - y, ___

if you're read - y. ___ I'm read - y. ___ If you're read - y, ___ if you're read - y, ___

we both know we ain't kids no more. ___

No, we ain't kids no more. ___

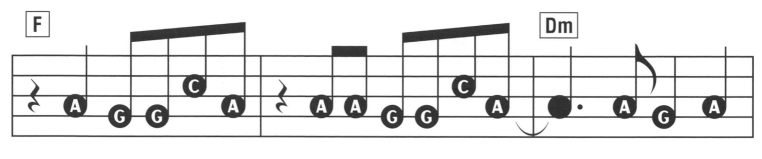

I'm giv - ing you up, I've for - giv - en it all, _____ you set me

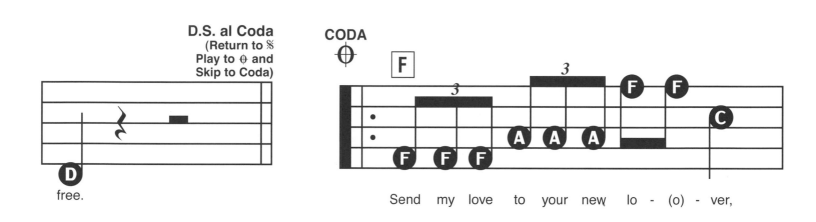

D.S. al Coda
(Return to %
Play to ⊕ and
Skip to Coda)

free.

CODA

Send my love to your new lo - (o) - ver,

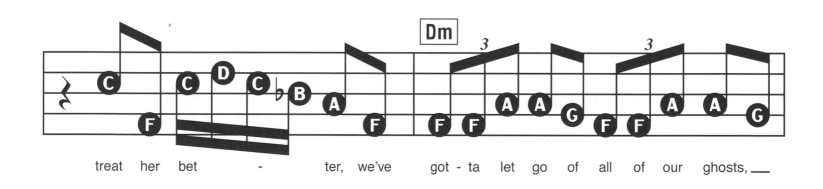

treat her bet - ter, we've got - ta let go of all of our ghosts, ___

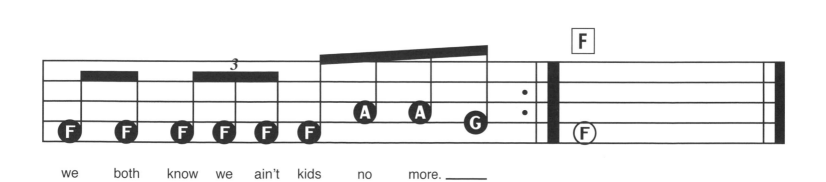

we both know we ain't kids no more. _____

7 Years

Registration 2
Rhythm: Rock or 8-Beat

Words and Music by Lukas Forchhammer,
Morten Ristorp, Stefan Forrest,
David Labrel, Christopher Brown
and Morten Pilegaard

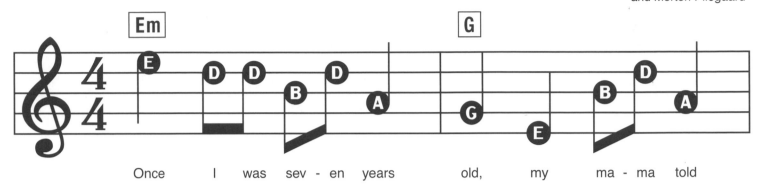

Once I was sev-en years old, my ma-ma told

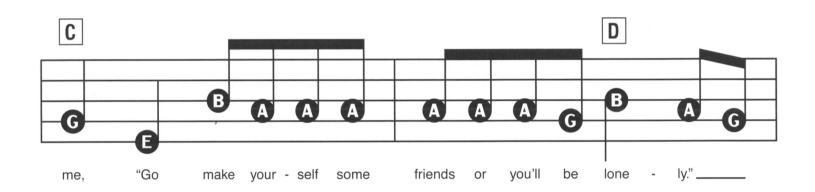

me, "Go make your-self some friends or you'll be lone-ly." _____

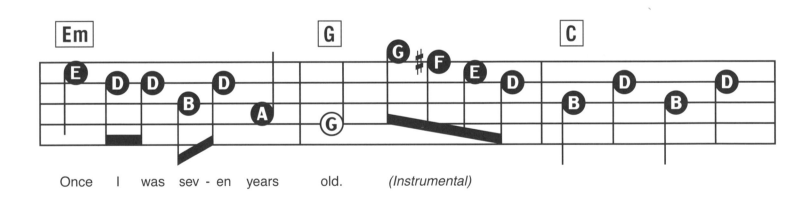

Once I was sev-en years old. (Instrumental)

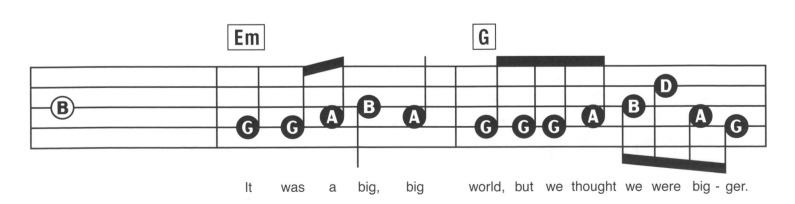

It was a big, big world, but we thought we were big-ger.

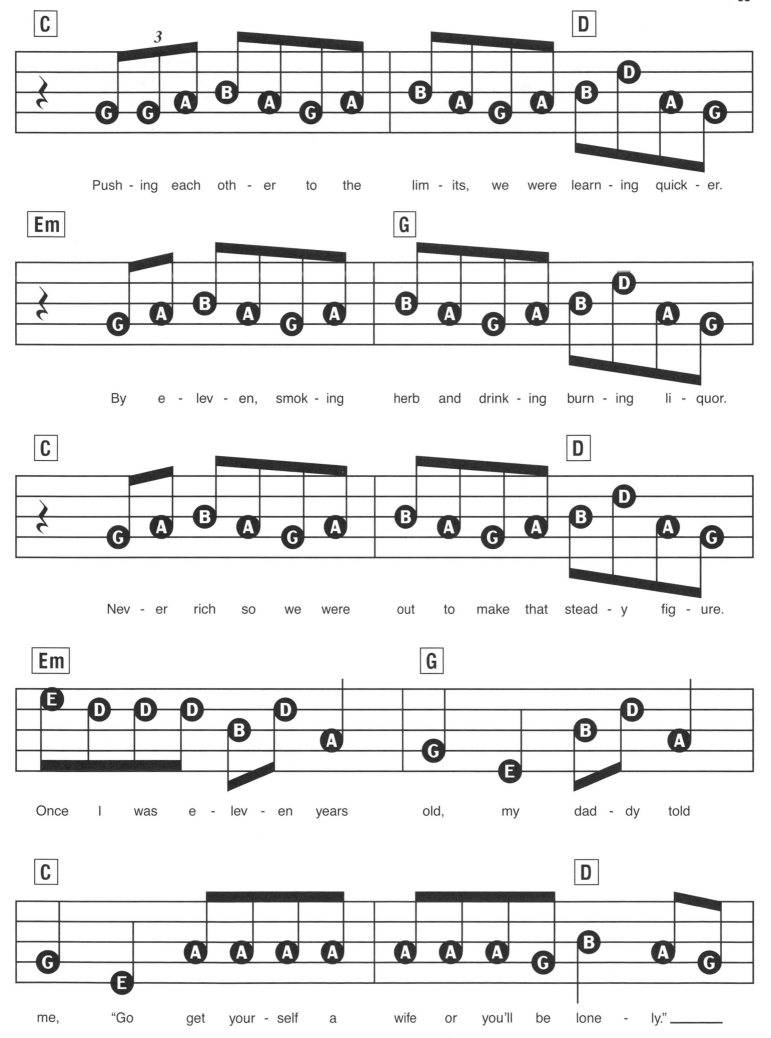

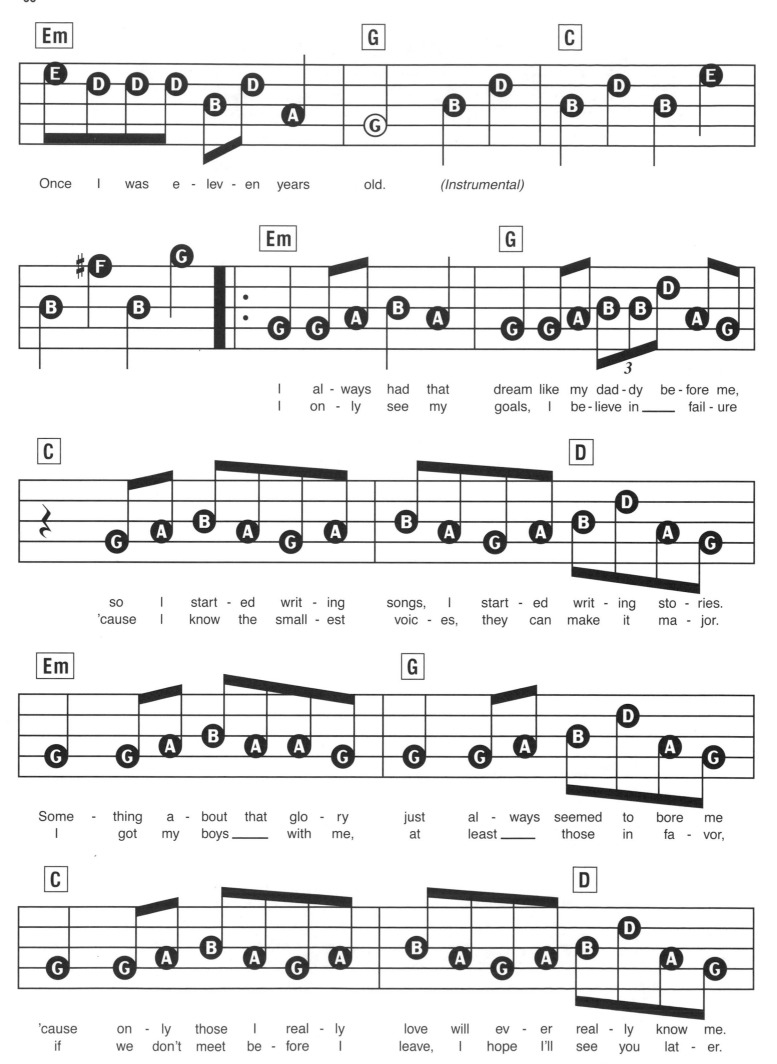

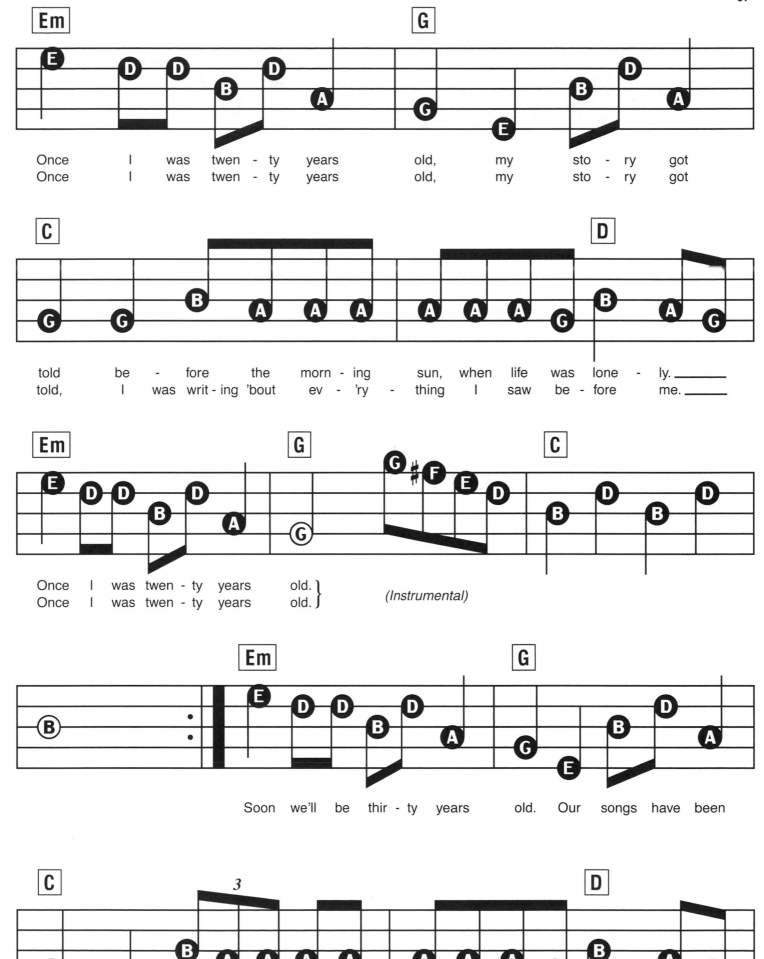

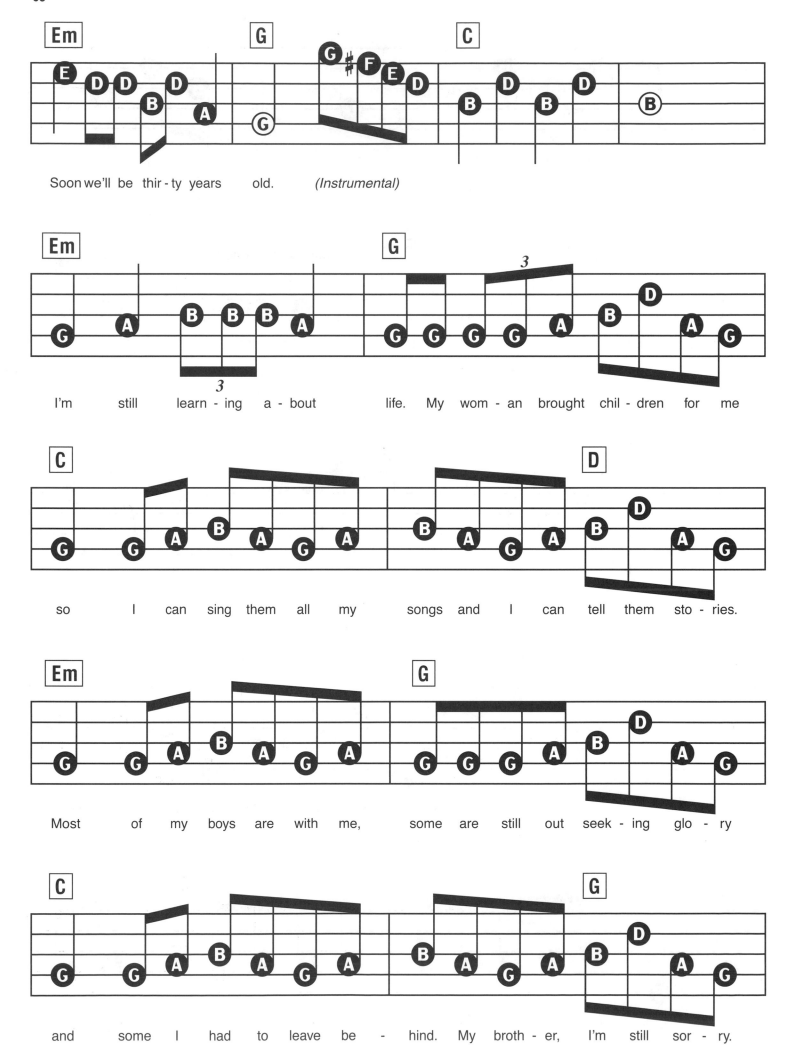

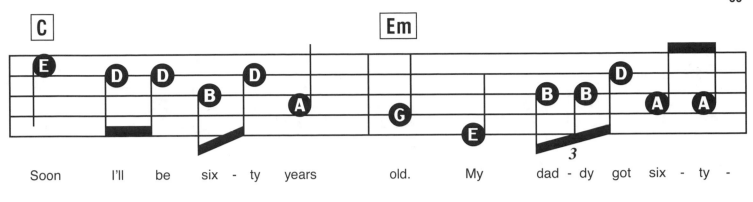

Soon I'll be six - ty years old. My dad - dy got six - ty -

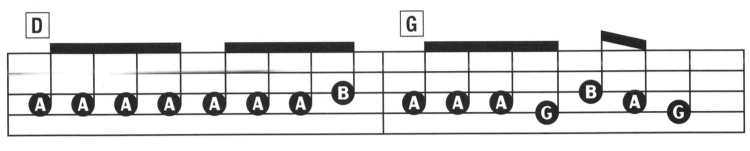

one. Re - mem - ber life and then your life be - comes a bet - ter one.

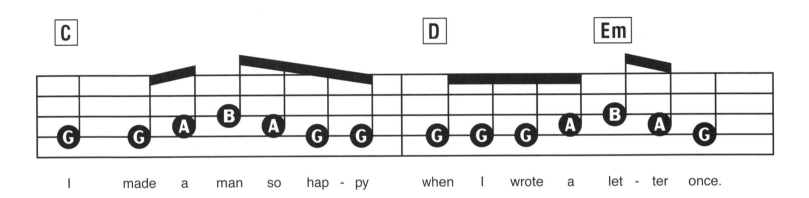

I made a man so hap - py when I wrote a let - ter once.

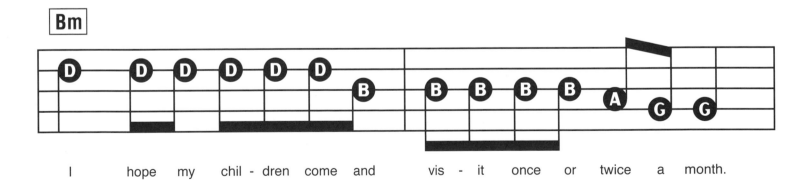

I hope my chil - dren come and vis - it once or twice a month.

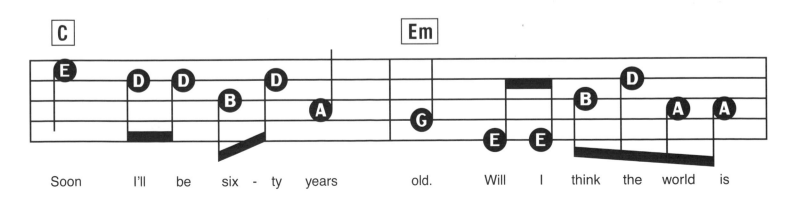

Soon I'll be six - ty years old. Will I think the world is

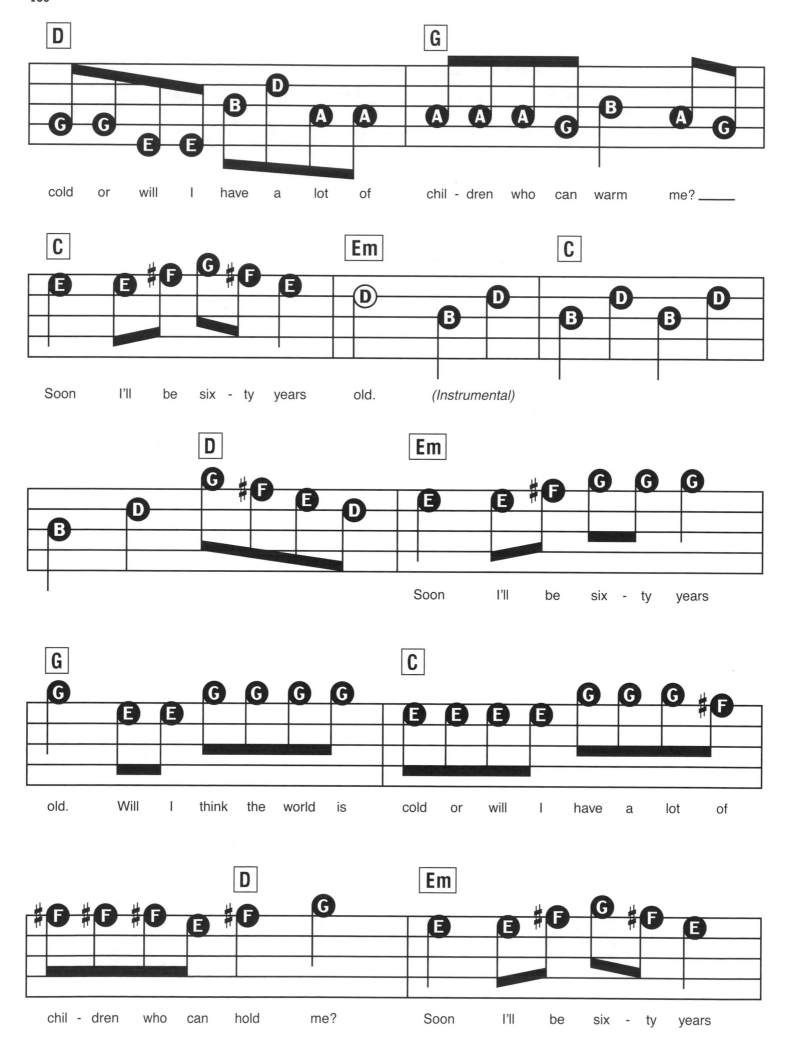

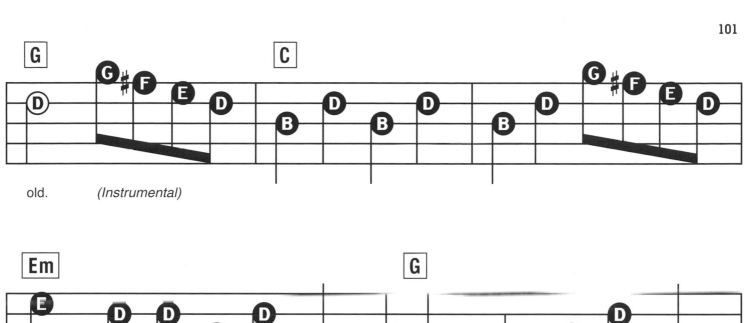

old.   *(Instrumental)*

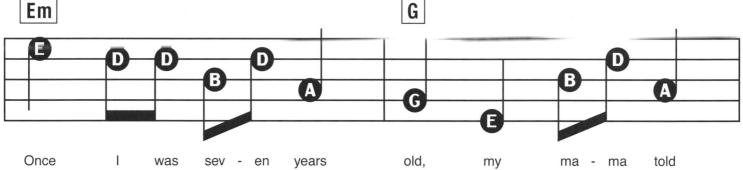

Once   I   was sev - en   years   old,   my   ma - ma   told

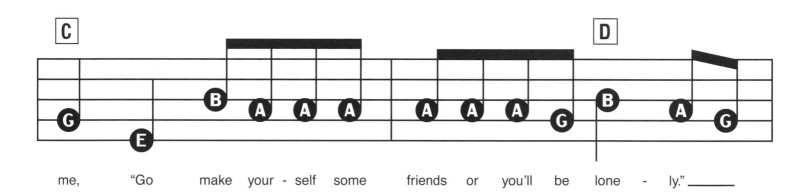

me,   "Go   make   your - self   some   friends   or   you'll   be   lone - ly." _____

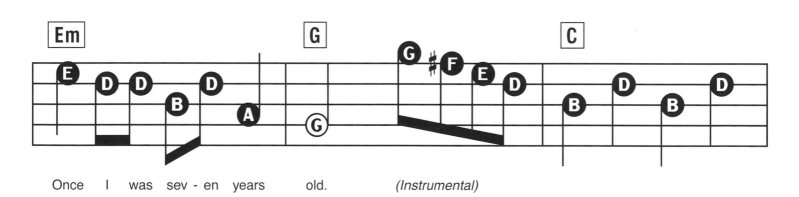

Once   I   was sev - en years   old.   *(Instrumental)*

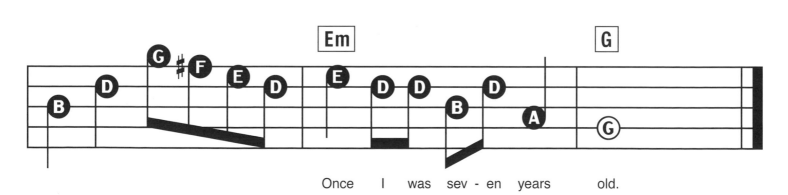

Once   I   was sev - en   years   old.

She Used to Be Mine
from WAITRESS THE MUSICAL

Registration 8
Rhythm: Waltz

Words and Music by
Sara Bareilles

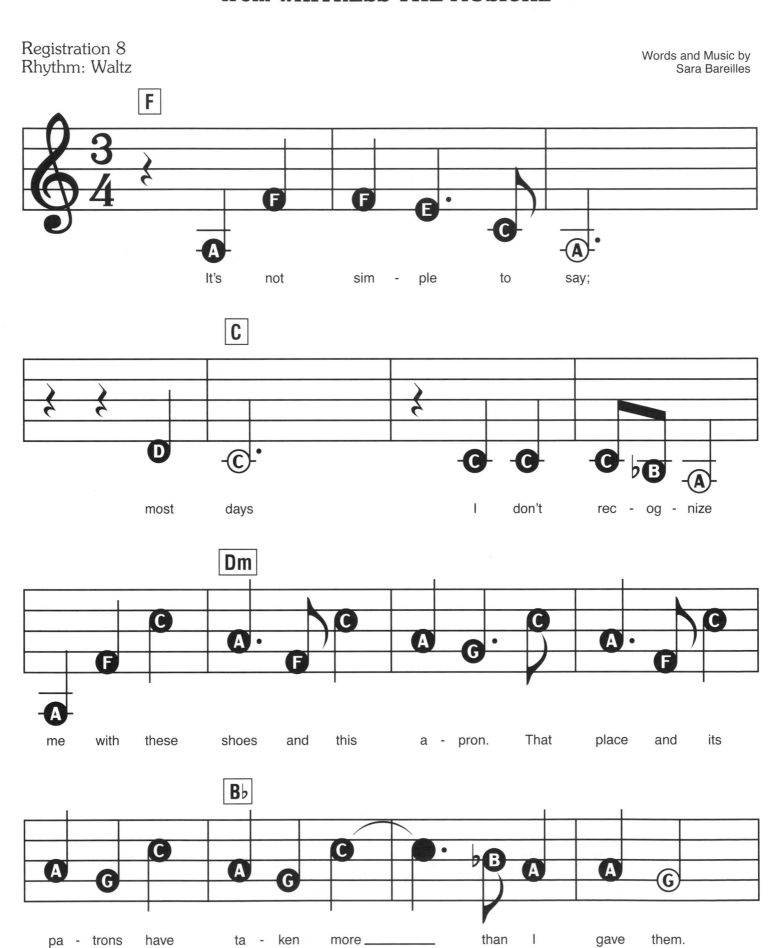

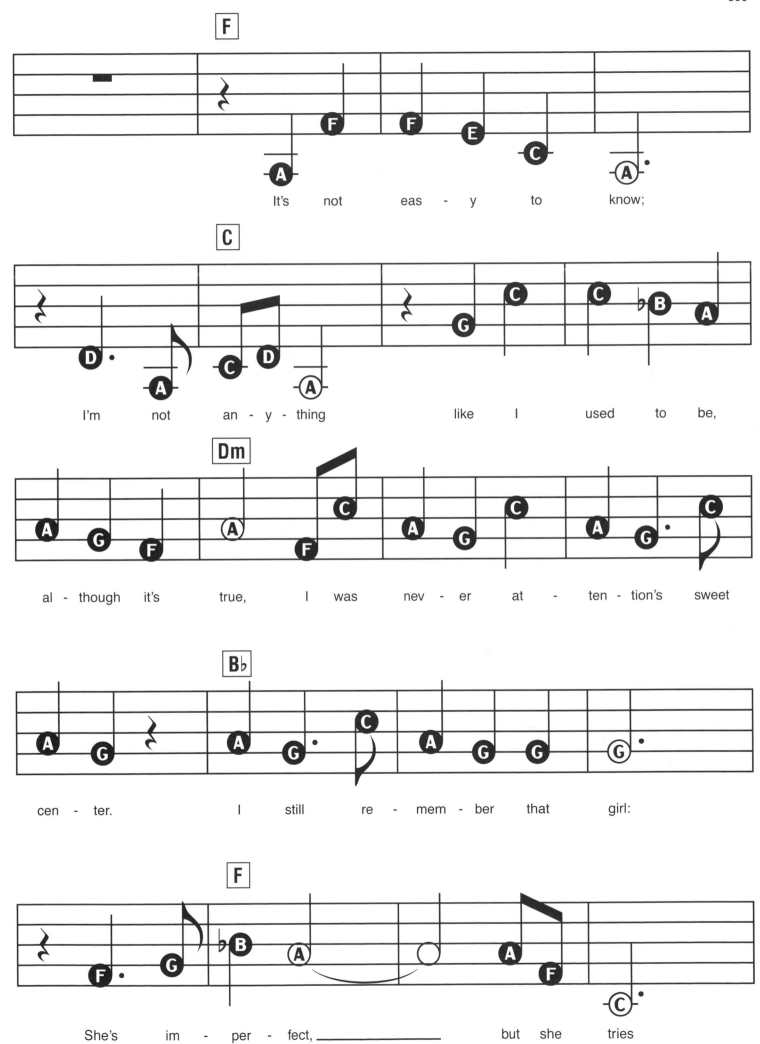

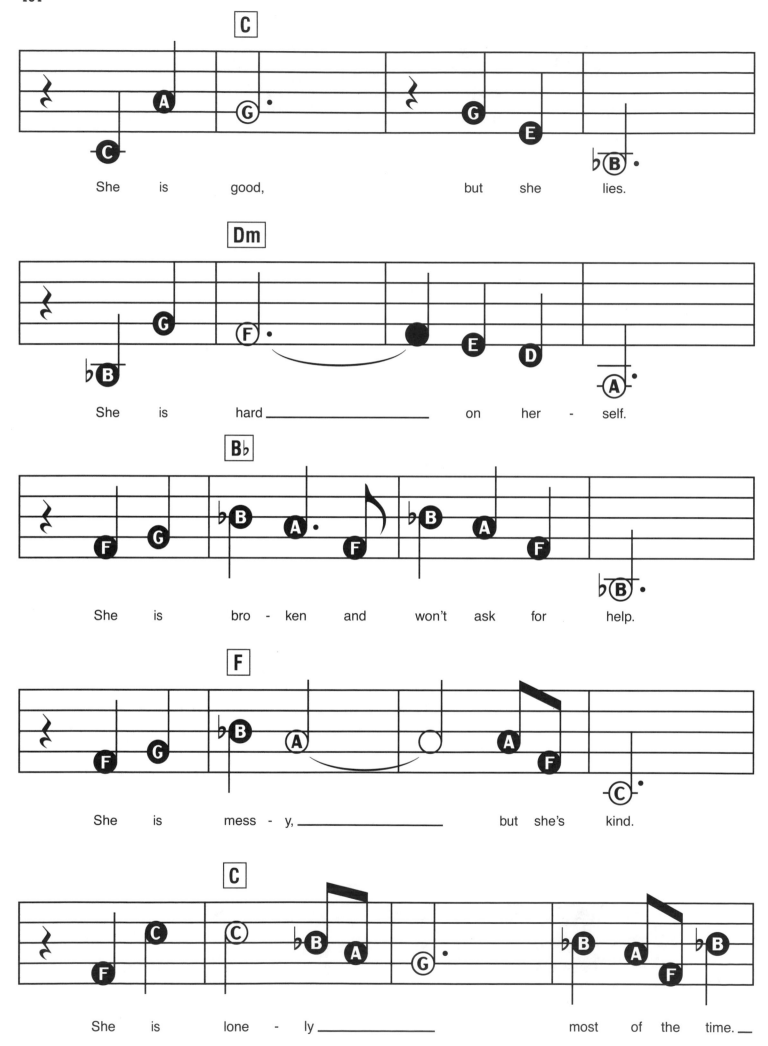

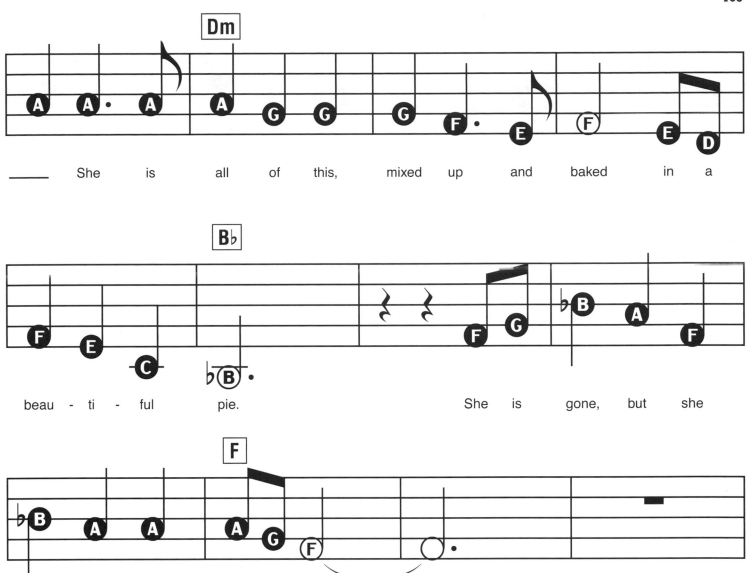

_____ She is all of this, mixed up and baked in a

beau - ti - ful pie. She is gone, but she

used to be mine. _____

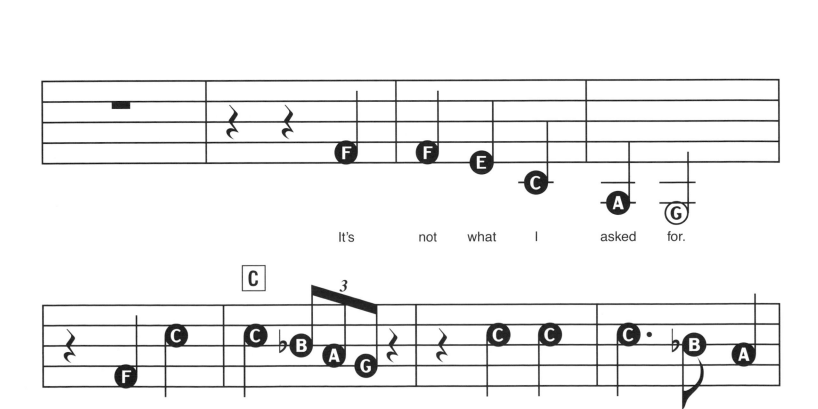

It's not what I asked for.

Some - times life _____ just slips in through a

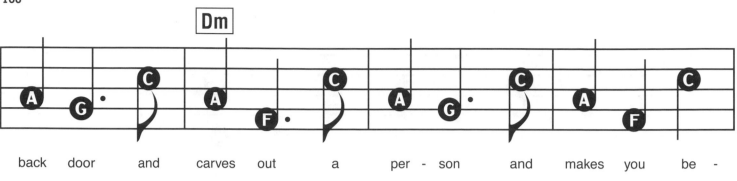

back door and carves out a per - son and makes you be -

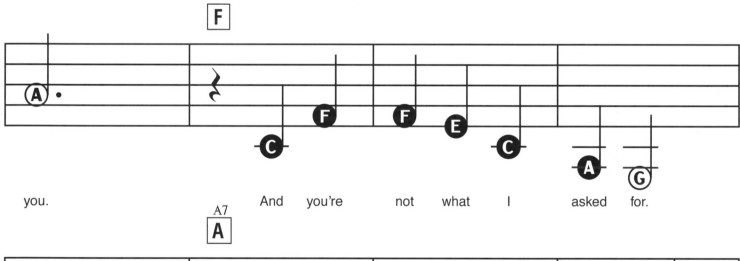

lieve it's all true, and now I've got

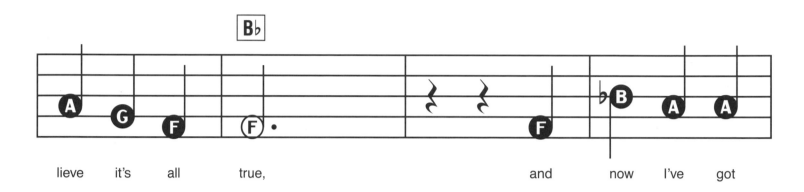

you. And you're not what I asked for.

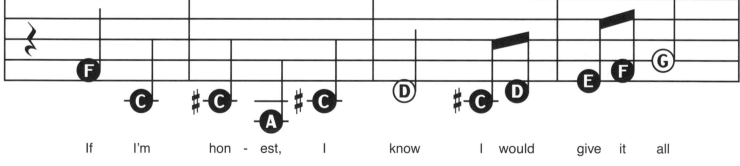

If I'm hon - est, I know I would give it all

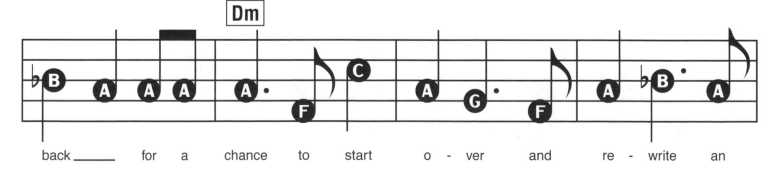

back _____ for a chance to start o - ver and re - write an

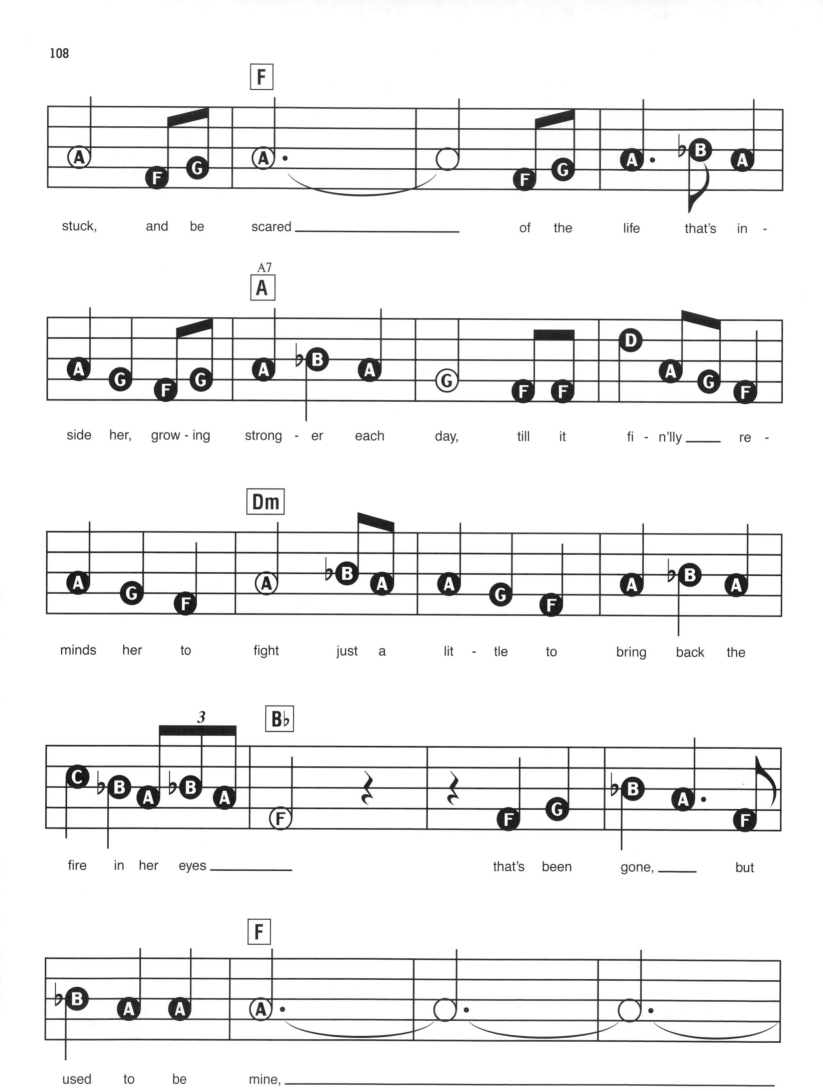

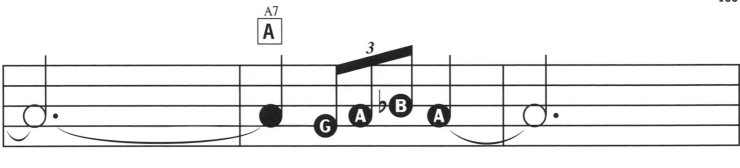

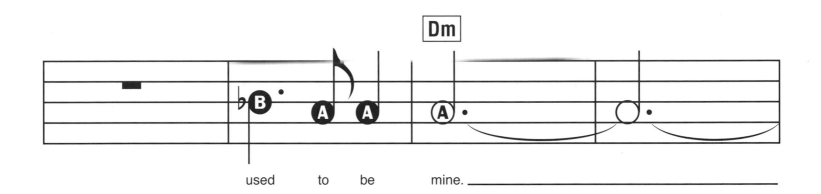

used to be mine. _____

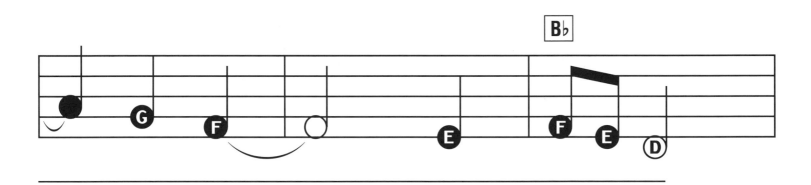

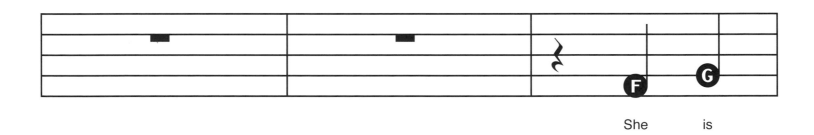

She is

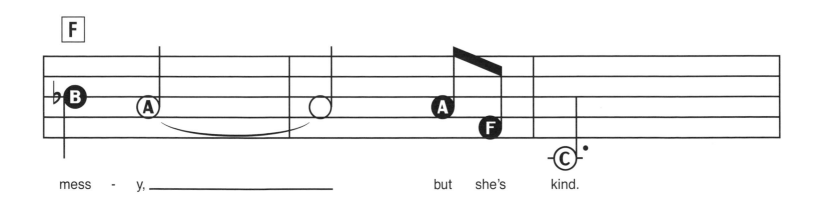

mess - y, _____ but she's kind.

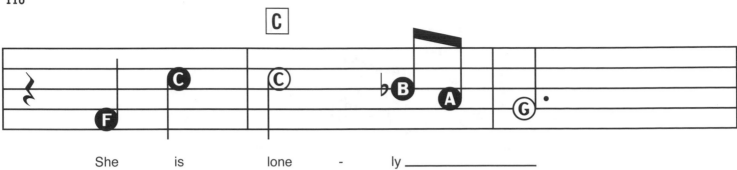

She   is   lone - ly _____

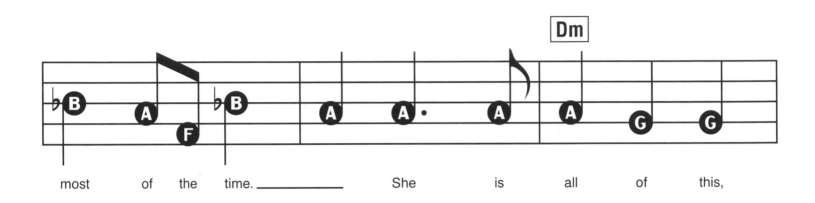

most   of   the   time. _____   She   is   all   of   this,

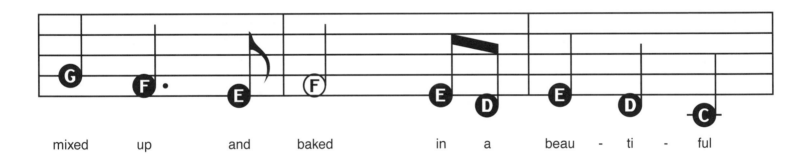

mixed   up   and   baked   in   a   beau - ti - ful

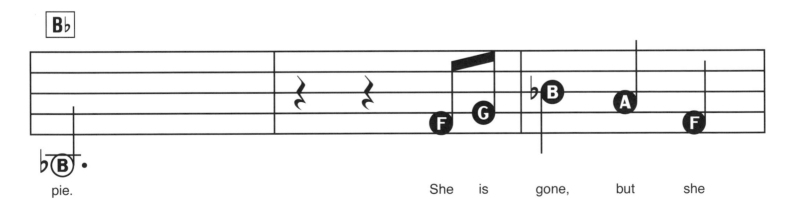

pie.   She   is   gone,   but   she

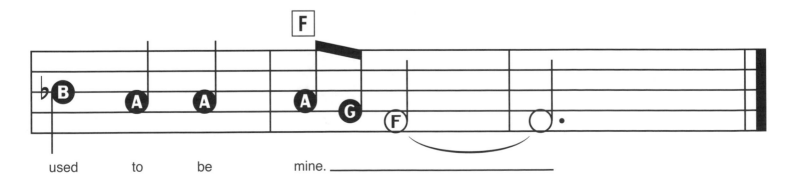

used   to   be   mine. _____

Tennessee Whiskey

Registration 9
Rhythm: Country

Words and Music by Dean Dillon
and Linda Hargrove

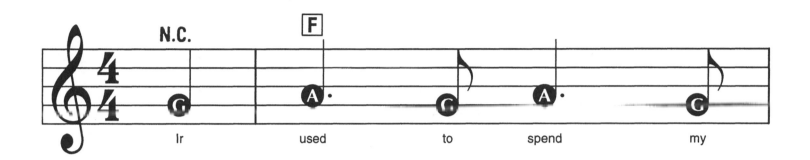

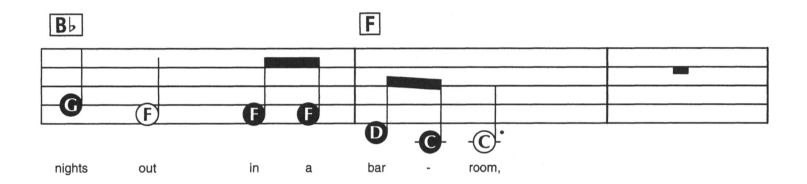

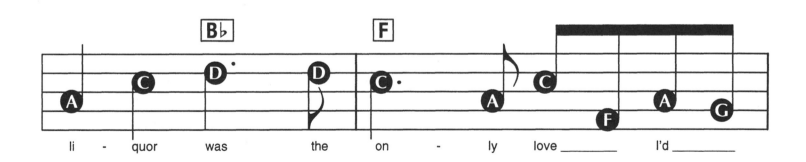

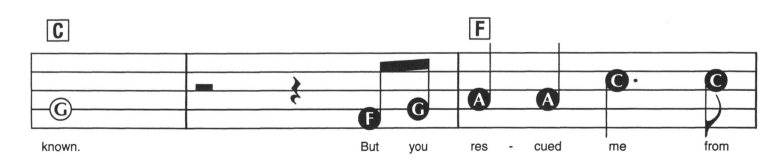

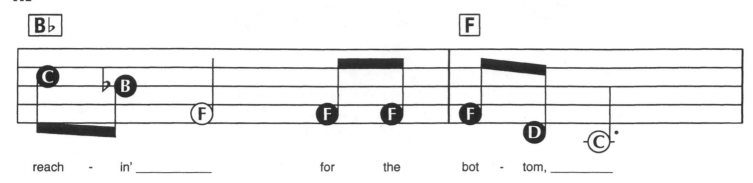

reach - in' _____ for the bot - tom, _____

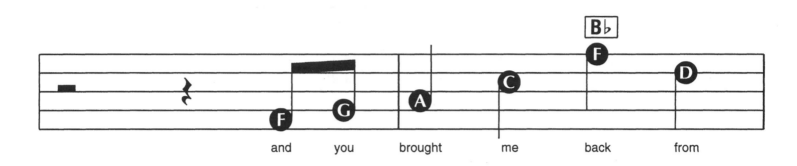

and you brought me back from

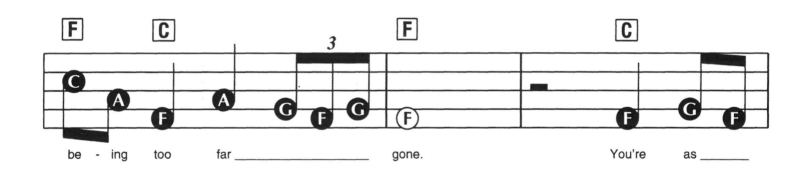

be - ing too far _____ gone. You're as _____

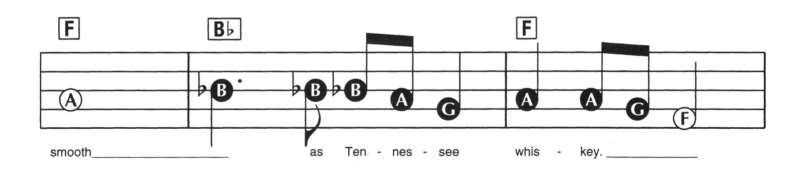

smooth_____ as Ten - nes - see whis - key. _____

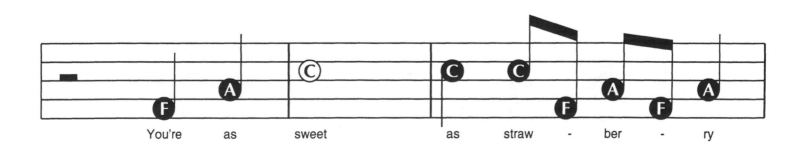

You're as sweet as straw - ber - ry

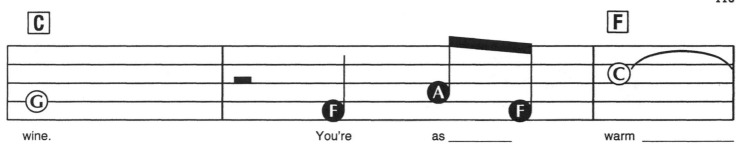

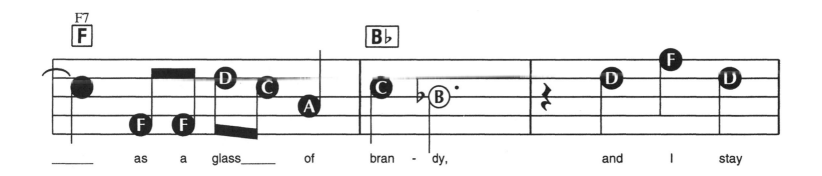

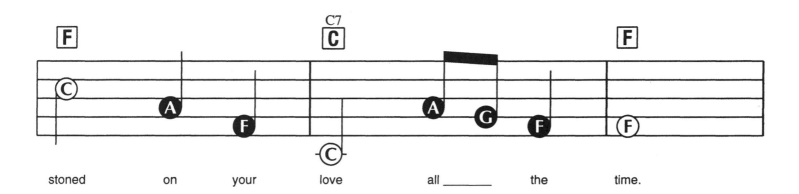

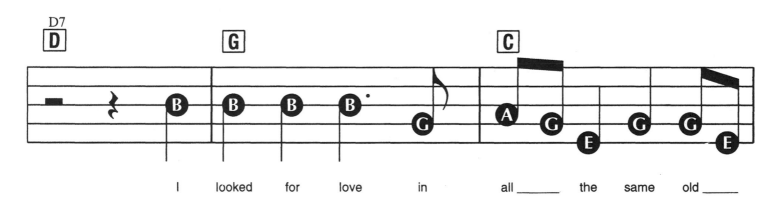

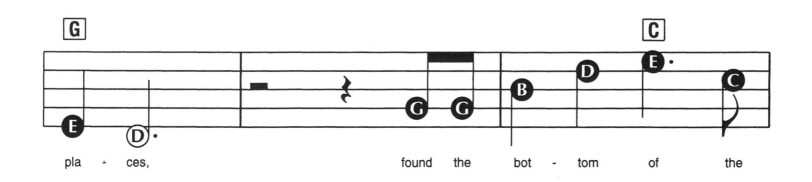

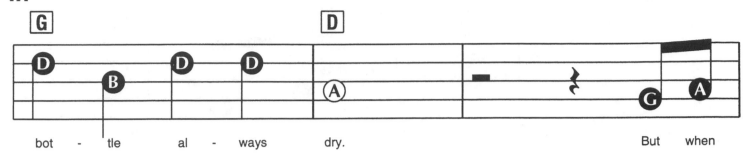

bot - tle al - ways dry. But when

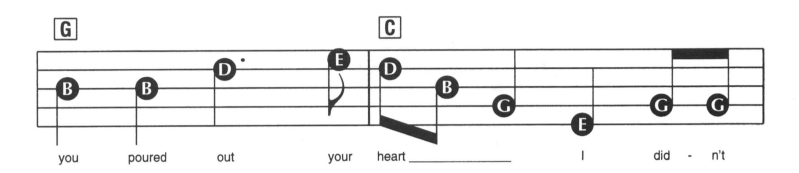

you poured out your heart _____ I did - n't

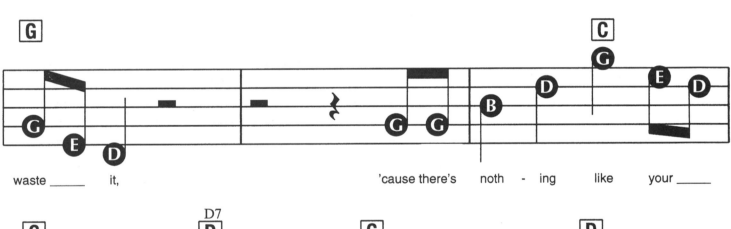

waste _____ it, 'cause there's noth - ing like your _____

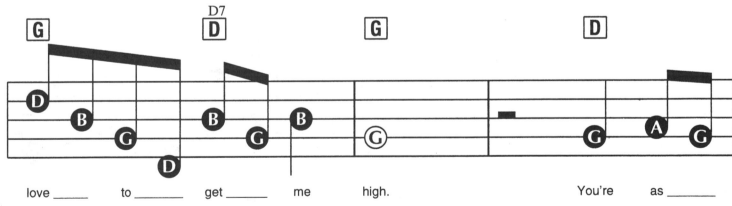

love _____ to _____ get _____ me high. You're as _____

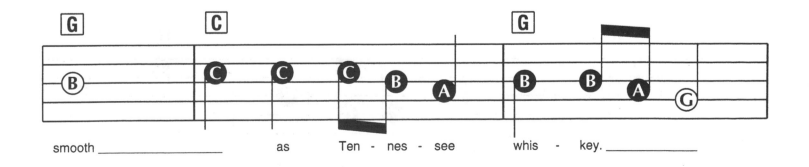

smooth _____ as Ten - nes - see whis - key. _____

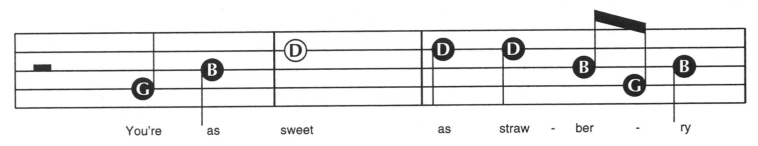

You're as sweet as straw - ber - ry

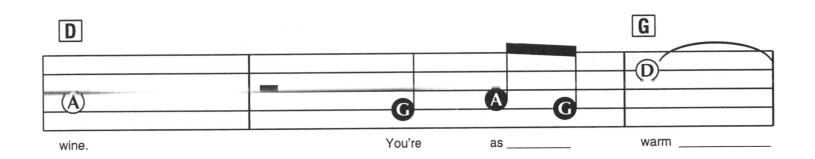

wine. You're as _____ warm _____

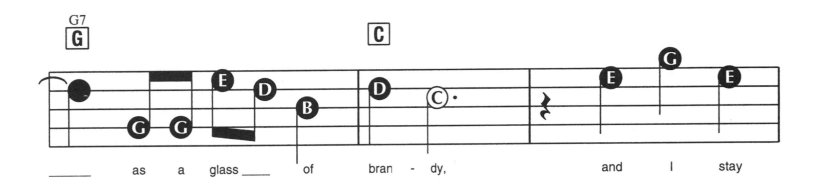

_____ as a glass ____ of bran - dy, and I stay

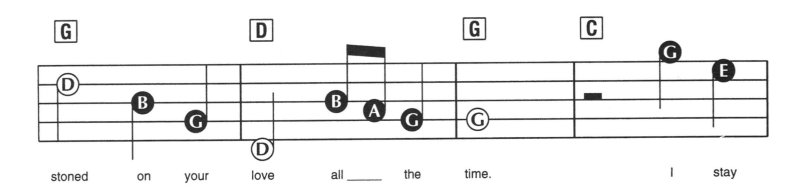

stoned on your love all ____ the time. I stay

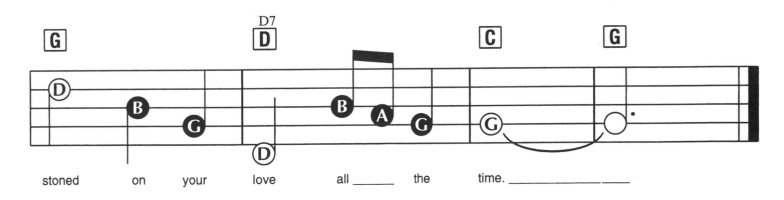

stoned on your love all _____ the time. _____

That's What I Like

Registration 8
Rhythm: Funk or Rock

Words and Music by Bruno Mars,
Philip Lawrence, James Fauntleroy,
Ray Charles McCullough II, Christopher Brody Brown,
Jeremy Reeves, Jonathan Yip and Ray Romulus

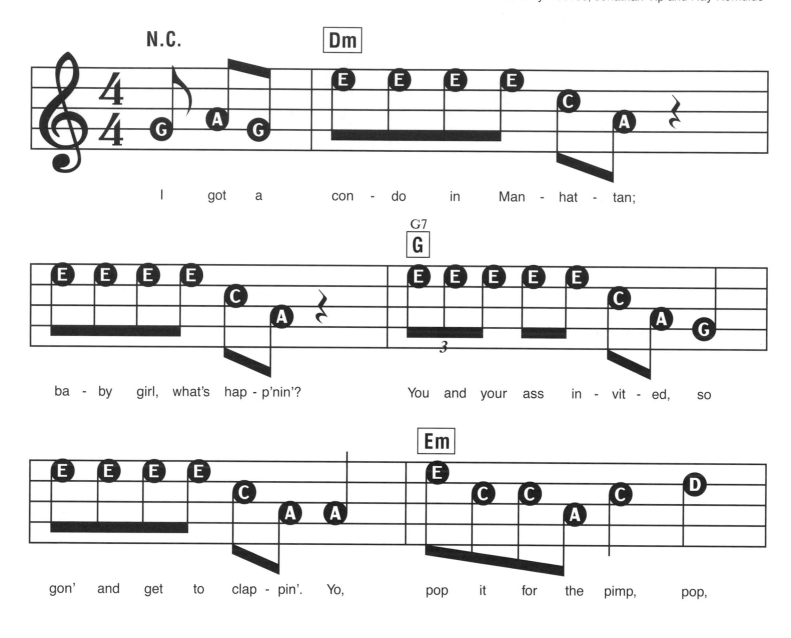

I got a con-do in Man-hat-tan;

ba-by girl, what's hap-p'nin'? You and your ass in-vit-ed, so

gon' and get to clap-pin'. Yo, pop it for the pimp, pop,

pop it for me. Turn a-round and drop it for a pimp, drop,

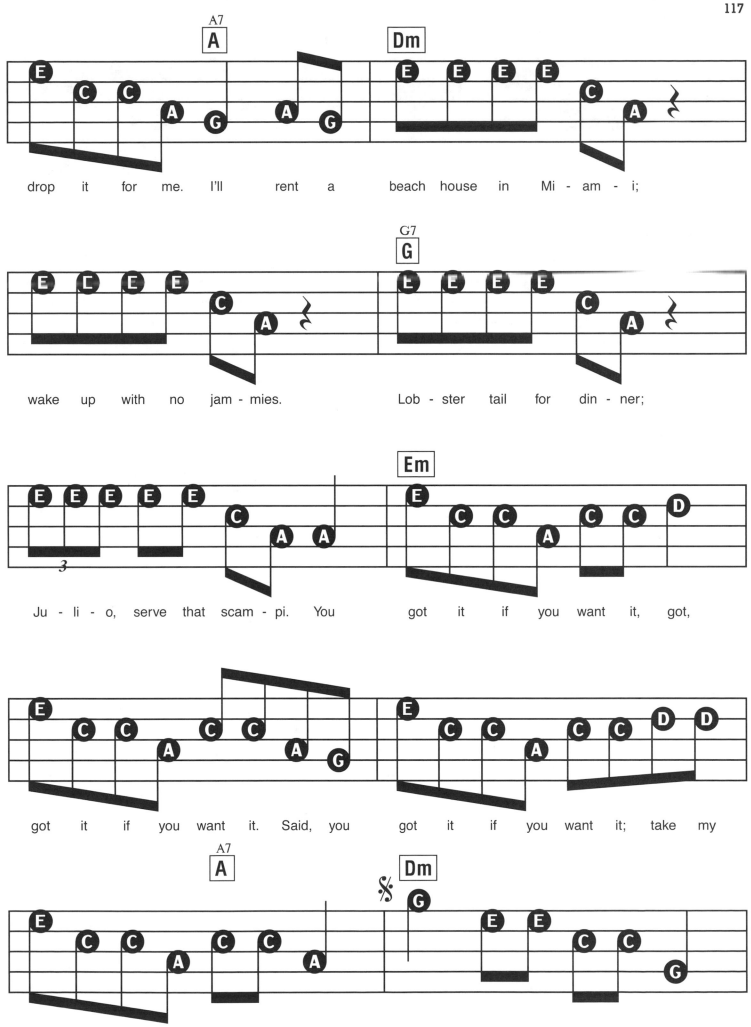

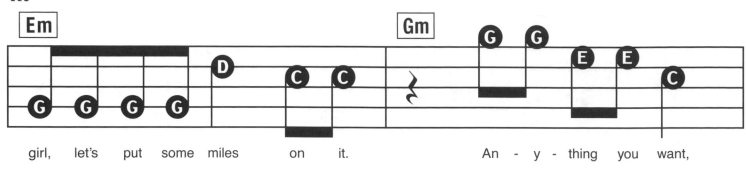

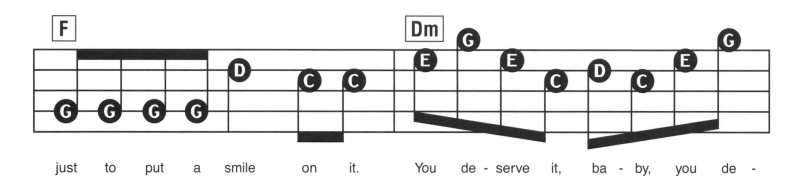

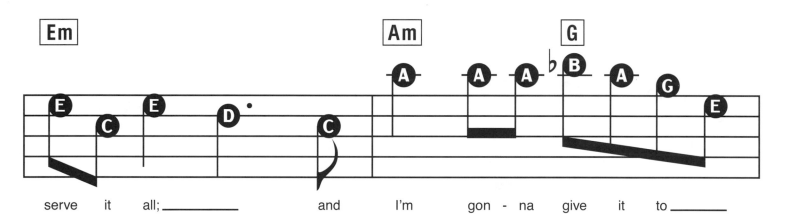

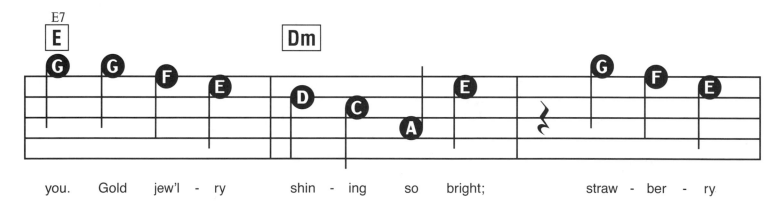

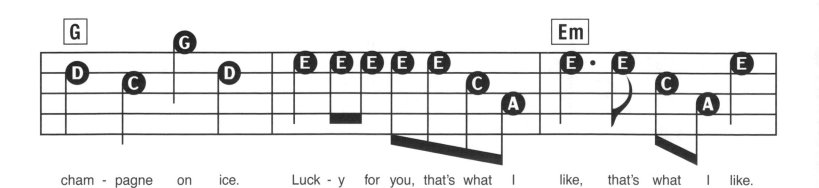

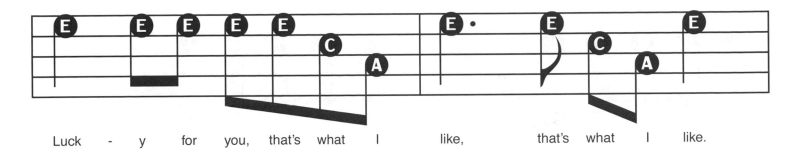

Luck - y for you, that's what I like, that's what I like.

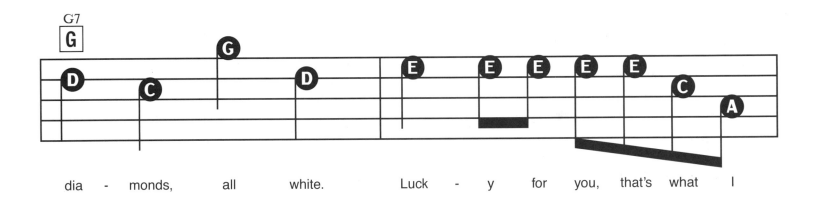

Sex by the fire _____ at night; silk sheets and

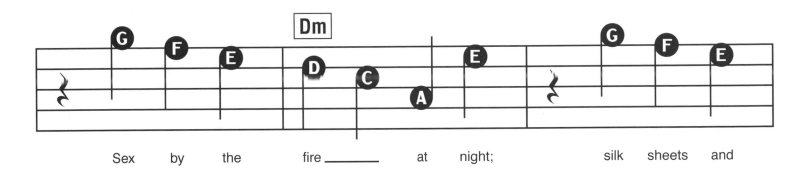

dia - monds, all white. Luck - y for you, that's what I

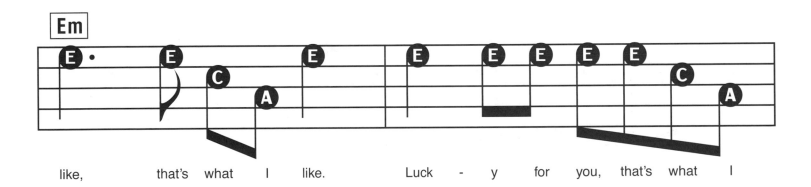

like, that's what I like. Luck - y for you, that's what I

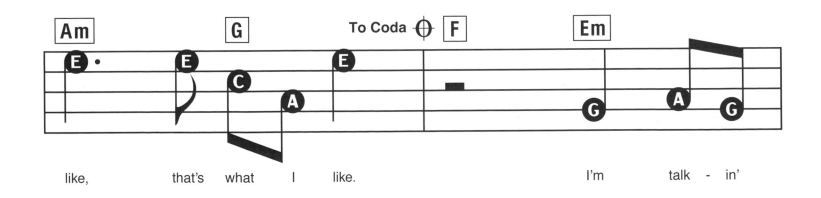

like, that's what I like. I'm talk - in'

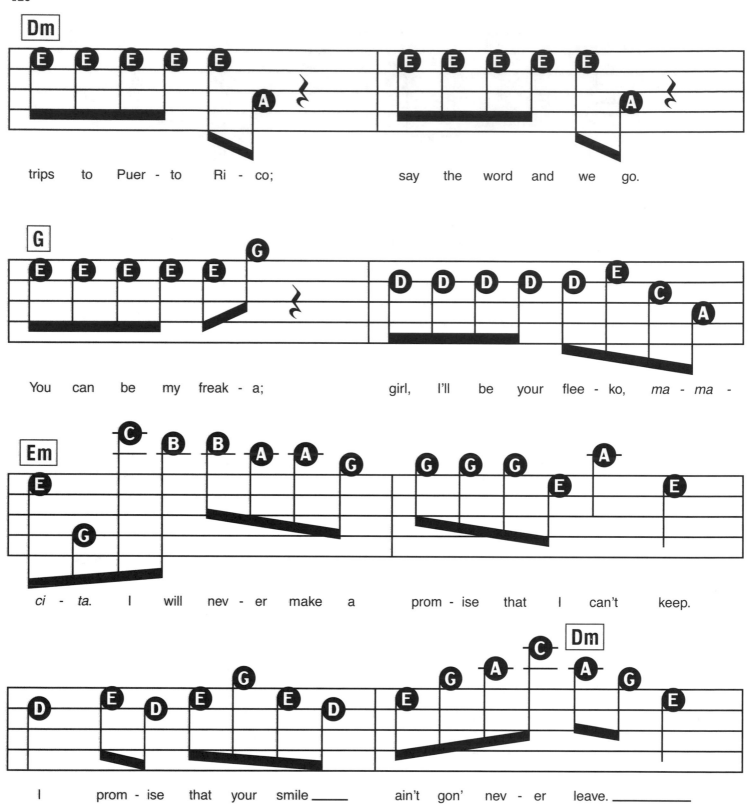

trips to Puer - to Ri - co; say the word and we go.

You can be my freak - a; girl, I'll be your flee - ko, *ma - ma -*

ci - ta. I will nev - er make a prom - ise that I can't keep.

I prom - ise that your smile ____ ain't gon' nev - er leave. _____

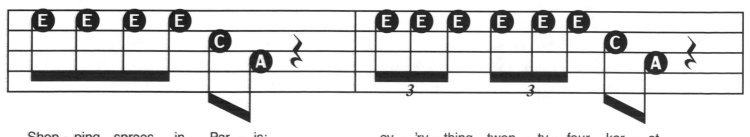

Shop - ping sprees in Par - is; ev - 'ry - thing twen - ty - four kar - at.

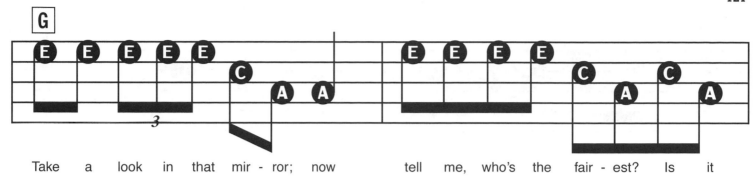

Take a look in that mir - ror; now tell me, who's the fair - est? Is it

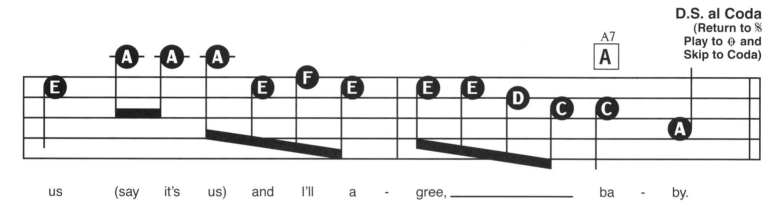

you? (Is it you?) Is it me? (Is it me?) Say it's

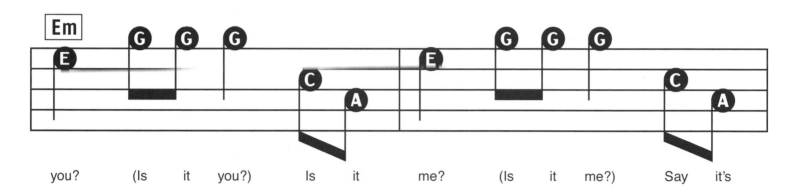

us (say it's us) and I'll a - gree, _____ ba - by.

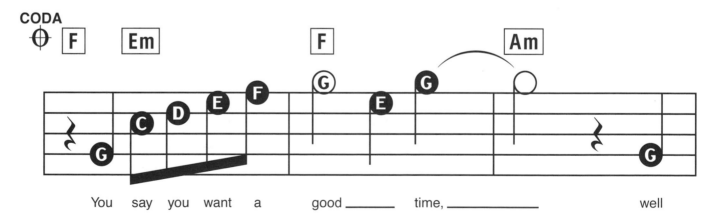

You say you want a good _____ time, _____ well

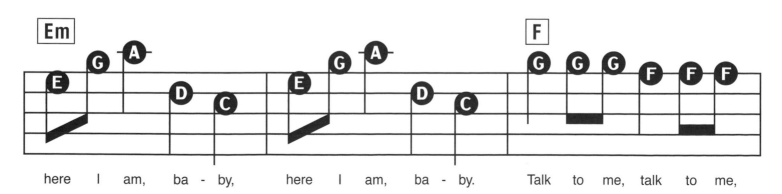

here I am, ba - by, here I am, ba - by. Talk to me, talk to me,

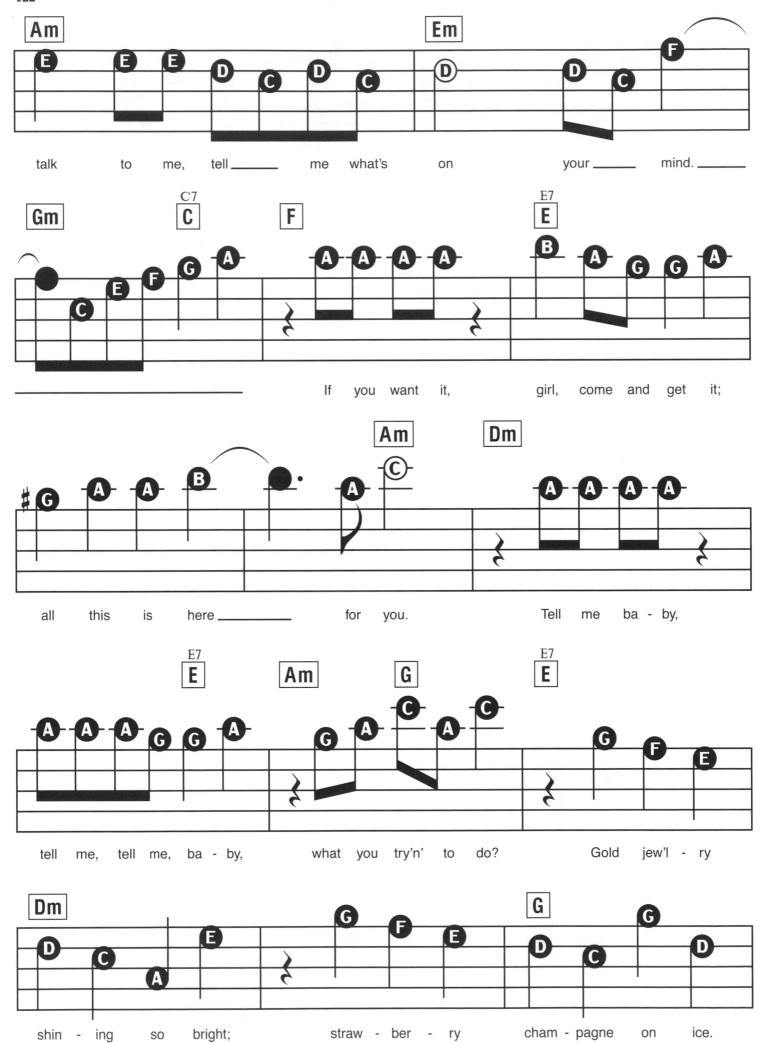

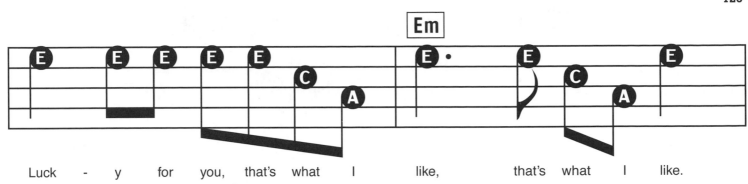

Luck - y for you, that's what I like, that's what I like.

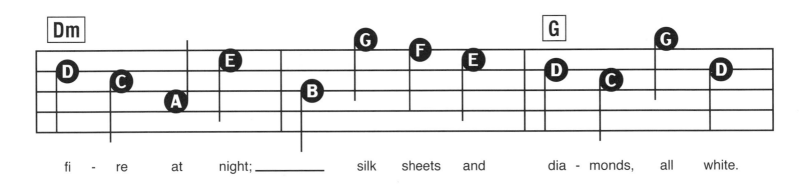

Luck - y for you, that's what I like, that's what I like. Sex by the

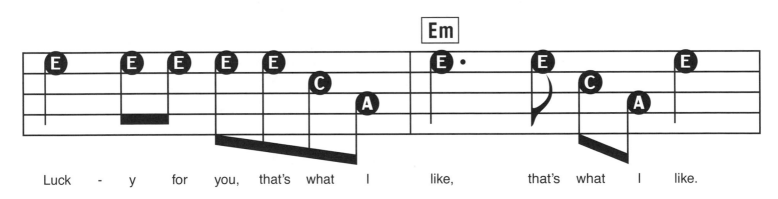

fi - re at night; _____ silk sheets and dia - monds, all white.

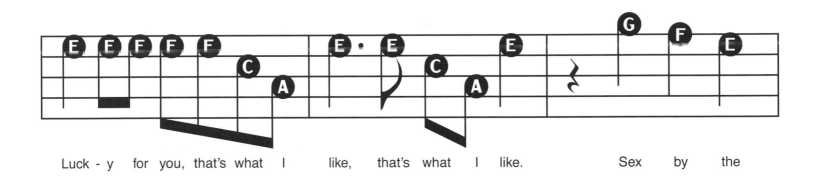

Luck - y for you, that's what I like, that's what I like.

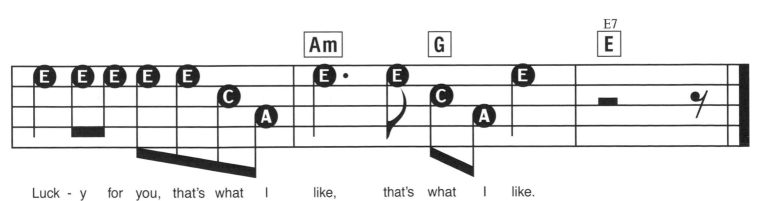

Luck - y for you, that's what I like, that's what I like.

Thinking Out Loud

Registration 4
Rhythm: 8-Beat or Rock

Words and Music by Ed Sheeran
and Amy Wadge

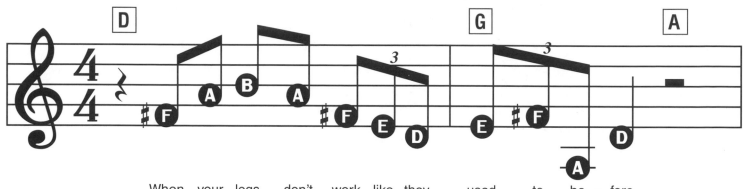

When your legs don't work like they used to be-fore
When my hair's all but gone and my mem-o-ry fades,

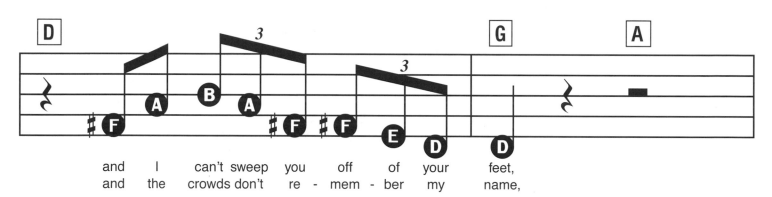

and I can't sweep you off of your feet,
and the crowds don't re-mem-ber my name,

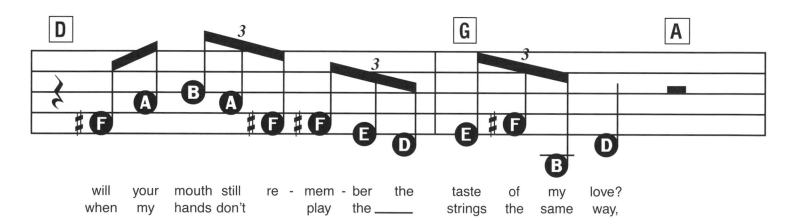

will your mouth still re-mem-ber the taste of my love?
when my hands don't play the _____ strings the same way,

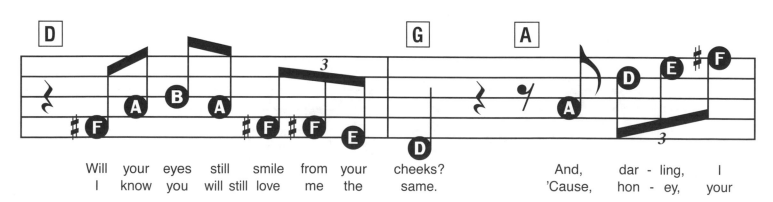

Will your eyes still smile from your cheeks? And, dar-ling, I
I know you will still love me the same. 'Cause, hon-ey, your

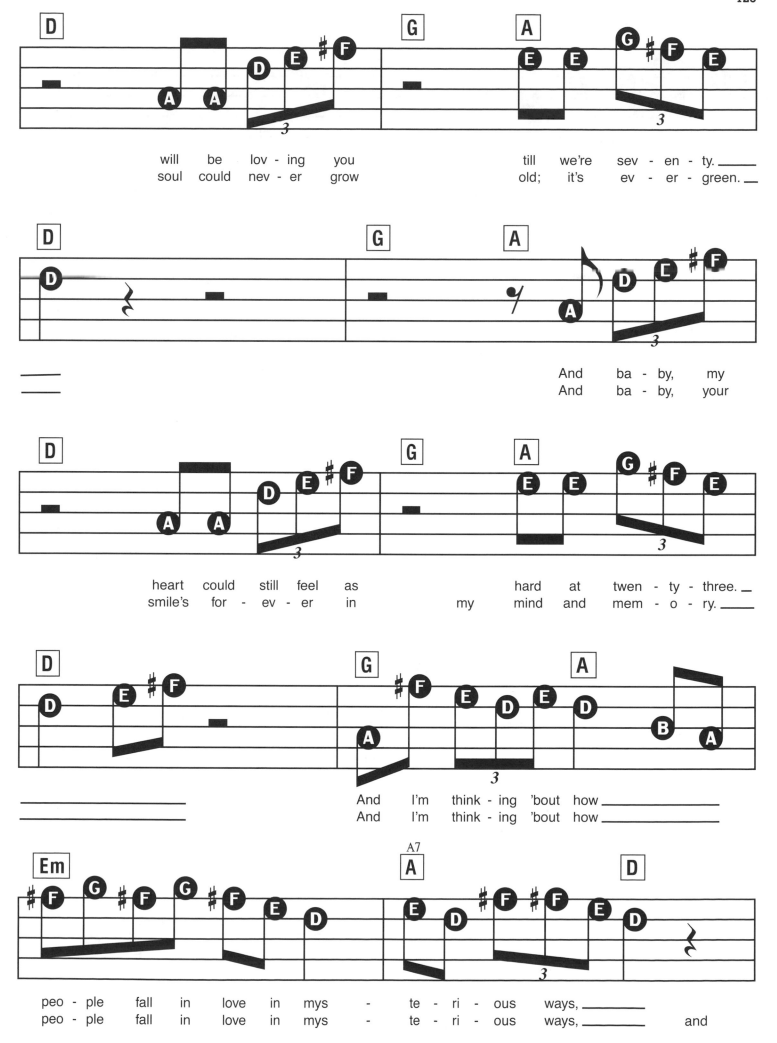

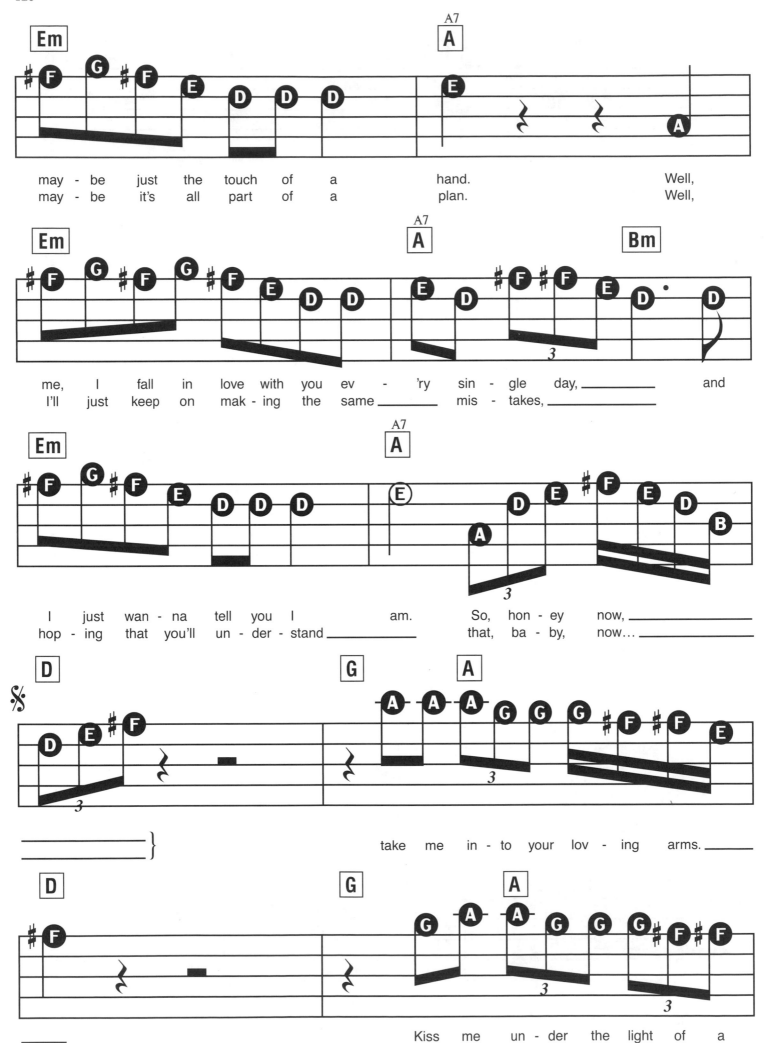

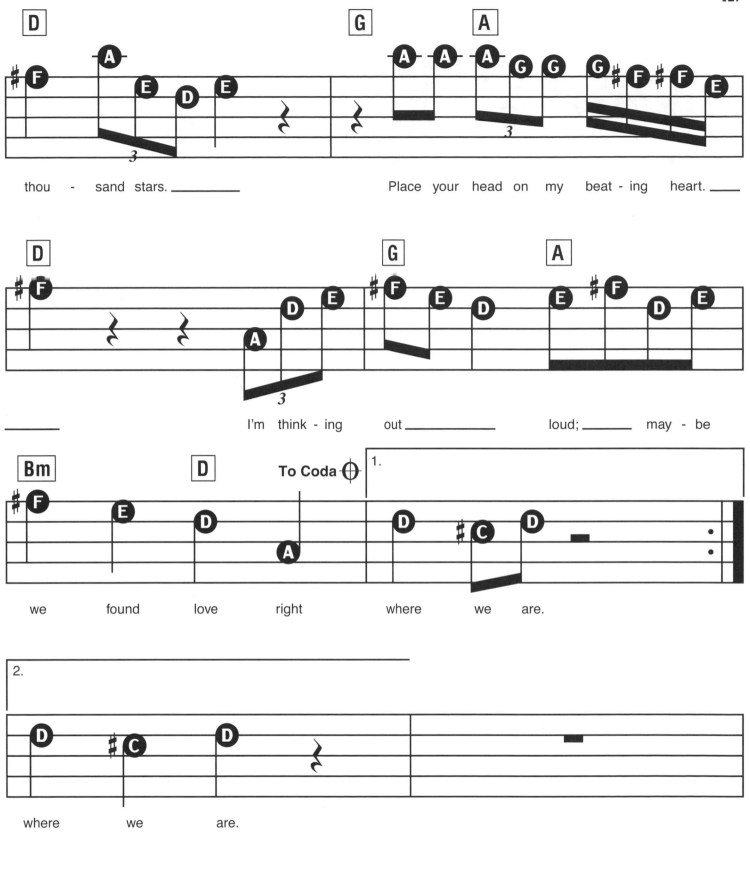

thou - sand stars. _____ Place your head on my beat - ing heart. _____

_____ I'm think - ing out _____ loud; _____ may - be

we found love right where we are.

where we are.

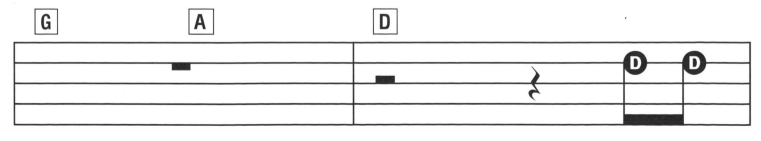

(La, la,

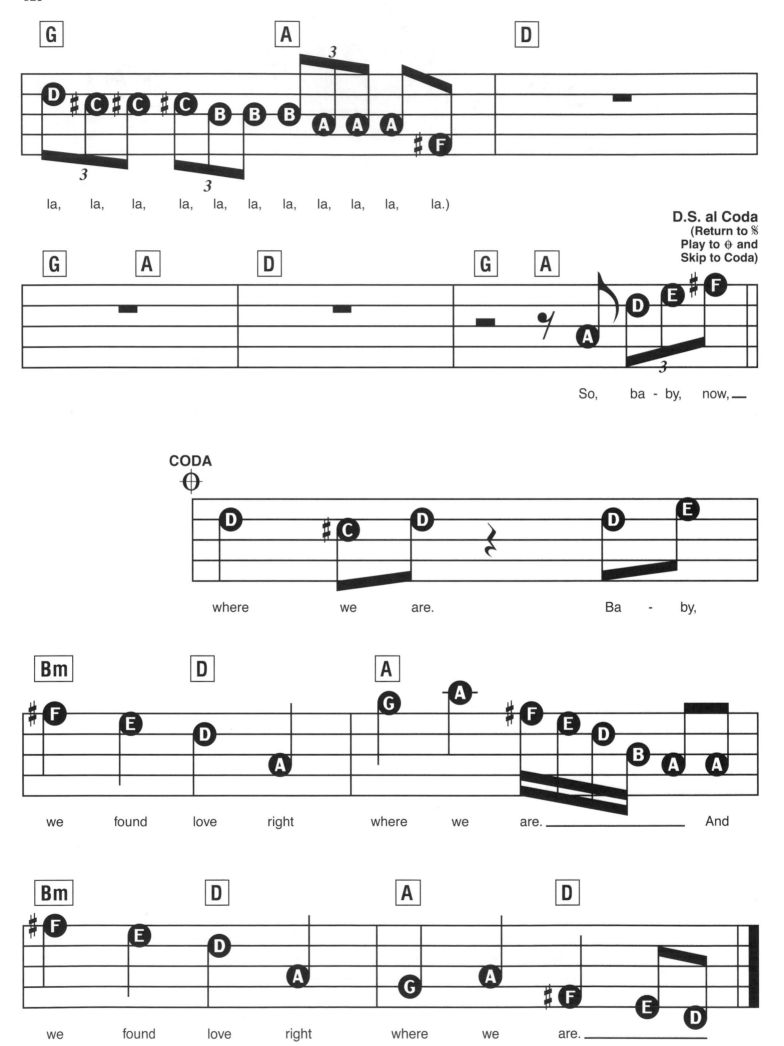